Time Ripples: A Gift of Love

Copyright © 2021 Robert H. Wellington

This book is a work of fiction. People, places, events, and situations are the products of the authors imagination. Any resemblance to persons, living or dead, or historical events, are purely coincidental.

All rights reserved. No part of this book may be reproduced, distributed, or transmitted in any form or by any means, including photocopying, recording, or other electronic or mechanical methods, without prior written permission from the publisher or author, except in the case of brief quotations embodied in critical reviews and certain other noncommercial uses permitted by copyright law.

Library of Congress Control Number	2021916355
Paperback	978-1-63626-987-0
Hardcover	978-1-63626-986-3
eBook	978-1-63626-985-6

Printed in the United States of America

FRISCO, TX 75034
United States

www.wa-publishing.com

Time Ripples

A Gift of Love

by
Robert H. Wellington

Robert H. Wellington

Foreword

I write for the children and we are all children

hoping that these words will have meaning for them

I write for the family and we are all one family

hoping that these thoughts may help our love flourish

I write for my brothers and sisters and we are all brothers and sisters

hoping these phrases will help us on our journey home

Prologue

These simple thoughts, poems and essays are presented with the hope that they stir something deep inside, helping each of us to reconnect with our inner voice or guide, a guide who waits silently and patiently to be recognized. A guide who waits in plain view if our eyes are clear, but is often hidden by the noise of the world. A guide, who in reality is our true self.

The truth is, illumination has already occurred. It does not reside in time and thus the world, which exists in time, cannot see it. Your Soul, however, is timeless. In deep silence our higher mind touches the Soul and in that instant all is revealed. That is why we all need to retire from the world from time to time and in quiet contemplation replenish ourselves. Nothing more needs to be done, for in putting Love first all else is taken care of. Kindness is the key. It is the energy of a harmonious life and there is no substitute for it. But just as electricity can be turned off by pulling a light switch, so this energy can be shut off by an unkind action, word, or thought. Without it our lives experience the traumas of the world. With it we experience harmony.

Always, however, we will be challenged. This is the Soul's way of hastening our journey home, as well as the journey of those traveling with us. Our responsibilities do not revolve around us alone but extend to all we come in contact with.

Many have often used these simple rules to meet the challenges confronting them. Some have seemed exhilarating. Some have seemed painful. But looking back all have accelerated their pace towards fuller understanding. Without periodic quiet moments to reflect on truth's meaning, life would be difficult indeed. With the light of quiet contemplation replenishing us, life is wonderful.

The journey when understood is a great joy. It seems long but it is not a journey of distance. It is a journey of mental adjustment. It is a journey of realization. Whether we know it or not, we are all taking this journey together. Some have gone before and have left clues to help us on our way. Some are traveling next to us and are there to help or be helped when we encounter difficult stretches of road. Others follow us and depend on the footprints that we leave to continue their progress. It is an endless procession, yet in very real terms we have already completed the journey, we have just failed (for now) to realize it.

We all have many gifts. The highest use we can put these gifts toward is to help others. The moment we share we receive. Giving hastens the journey and with each giving act a joyous cry is heard in heaven. Have you ever felt shivers after experiencing (giving or receiving) a kindness, or a breakthrough thought? I often think of these as cheers from heaven. With each breakthrough, the world becomes a little brighter and you and all those who shared the experience with you are a little closer to realizing that which your Soul already knows.

Robert H. Wellington

Table of Contents

Foreword i
Prologue iii
New from Old 1
The Father 2
Whispers 3
Both Flower and Thorn 4
Civilization 6
Recognize 7
Gentle One 8
Love Made Manifest 9
The Purpose (A Prayer) 10
Thoughts 11
The Search 12
Fleeting 13
Good Deeds 14
Find It, Share It, Let It Grow 15
Breakthrough 16
Silence 17
Open the Gate 18
Love 19
Gentle Flower 20

A Journey in Dream Space 21

Freedom Within 24

Within 25

I See You 26

The Presence 27

Follow It Within 28

Become The Sculptor 29

Silent Roar 30

Within My Heart 31

Seeking 32

Becoming 33

Transforming Power 34

And So It Begins 35

A Higher Sense 36

Soul Mates Journey – A Young Girl's Cry 37

Life 38

Beginnings 39

Finding Clarity 40

To a Loving Mother – God Bless You Mom 41

A Childs Song 42

Clear the Way 43

Fear 44

The Quest 46

I Say In My Heart	47
God's Smile	48
I Give, I Love, and Therefore, I Am	49
Becoming	50
As A Man Thinketh	51
Heaven On Earth	52
The Family	54
Soul Mates	55
In the Quiet	56
Beyond	57
The Promise and Gift	58
As It Should Be	59
Start Now	60
Soaring	61
Silence in Chaos	62
The Journey's Song	63
Partake of Love's Joy	64
Only One Way	65
Small Steps Home	66
So Little Time	67
Shine Forth	68
Loving Footsteps	69
The Song of Joy	70

Shedding Anchors	71
The Journey	72
A Pilgrim in Hiding	73
Joy	75
Love and Know	76
Children	77
Liquid Silence	78
Silent Moments	79
Thoughts for a Beloved Son	80
Loves My Need	82
God Bless the Listeners	83
Levels We Have Traveled	84
Thoughts on Life	85
I Am You	87
Kindness	88
In the Eyes of A Child	89
A Call for Peace	90
Thoughts for a Beloved Daughter	92
That Easy and That Hard	94
Inspiration	95
Balance	96
From the Mountain Top	97
All Are Family	98

All from You (A Prayer) 99

The Choice is Ours 100

The Source 103

Drumbeats 104

Peace 105

A Marriage Blessing 106

Innocence 108

A Life Well Lived 110

Never Alone 111

Timeless 112

Water and Love 113

Forgiving 114

Relinquishing the Throne 115

In the Silence 116

Free Yourself From Restrictions 117

The Prayer and the Answer 118

Spirit 119

Flickering Light 120

Wonder 121

Surrender 122

Full Participation 123

Giving 124

Quickening 125

The Heart	126
Fear	127
The Battle	128
Stillness	129
Love the Creator	130
Renewal	131
To the Children	132
Growing Up	133
Appreciation	134
Attraction	135
The Gift of Giving	136
Homeward Bound	137
The Way of the Heart	138
The Razor's Edge	139
Children	140
Teen Years	141
Sleeping and Awakening	142
Quiet	143
The Search	144
Wilderness Morning	145
Charge Us with Your Holy Spirit	146
Surrender	147
His Gift	148

God Bless this Journey 149

Destroying Evil 150

Guidance 151

Filling Emptiness 152

Whispers – I am Never Alone 153

Timelessness 154

Sing Your Song 155

See Him 156

The Pain of Compassion 157

Thoughts 158

Robert H. Wellington

New from Old

With craggy trunk and branches old
It sits and watches life unfold
Life's end is near, deep wisdom shows
It longs to share that which it knows
It cannot speak and yet it gives
To those who see, to those who live
A life that's hard, has left its mark
It leaves its fruit to fill the dark
For there upon a tired branch
A perfect apple there to grasp
Life's lesson there for all to see
New comes from old, the living tree
For when the old is reabsorbed
New life continues in its fold

The Father

The child sees Him standing tall
There to protect from fear, from all
He intercedes when help is right
He urges on when growth is bright
He loves the family, seeing there
The glow of God from everywhere
He strives to do what's best, what's right
He tries but deep inside the fight
Rages between light and dark
Rages between void and spark
He's just a man but through His love
He hopes for guidance from above
He looks to God to hold His hand
To lead the children to gentle lands

Whispers

Whispers soft and subtle flow through all that exists

Telling of His glory and that which is His gift

Hidden by the chaos and glamour of this world

The whispers and their message, too often are not heard

Internally the whispers call out to those who hear

To those where quiet reigns

To those who have no fear

Behind all of creation Behind the manifest

Behind the subtle worlds of truth

They call us to the quest

Both Flower and Thorn

Have you ever observed on a sunny morn,
How the light embraces both flower and thorn?
How the breeze caresses all with its touch.
Quaking leaves and pine needles everything such,
That none are neglected and all feel his love.
From the least to the greatest, smallest insect to dove.
Mighty rivers and oceans to dew on a leaf.
All are touched with his goodness to the world's great relief.
All encompassed in light, all a part of the whole.
Each an integral player and each with its role.
Only one need be absent and his plans incomplete.
All must be in the picture before we can meet,
The truth at the beginning where we started our quest.
There it was all along deep inside of our breast.
We were lost in a world that we made with our thoughts.
A world filled with comparing and the pain that it brought.

Robert H. Wellington

Where there's better and worse where there's new and there's old.

Where there's black and there's white, where there's lead and there's gold.

He sent light and it brightened all that it touched.

Laying answers before us, a guide giving much.

Quietly waiting for someone to see.

That the truth is a oneness of you and of me.

And the world of comparing disappears in its glow.

For the light has revealed we're all part of his flow.

Nothing better nor worse, nothing plain nor so fair.

For we're nothing lest he shines within each to share

Separate bodies we see; separate forms show their face.

But our minds are connected with his holy grace.

So to live life in joy, knowing earth, sky and sea.

Let truth un-fold within you so abundantly,

Pain once falsely embraced, never there, now has ceased.

And your heart now knows love and your soul now knows peace.

Civilization

Civilizations are born by the will of God but they die by the will of man. Only the living truth is eternal. Man in his attempts to hold on to the physical, crystallizes civilization in its institutions and laws. He steadfastly tries to hold on to the status quo, thus suffocating the living truth which first brought the civilization into being. Crystallization is the forerunner of death. The living truth must grow so that the old is constantly refreshed and renewed.

Recognize

Recognize His will as your will and life unfolds before you in all its beauty and grandness.

Recognize His love as your love and the treasure house of heaven opens its doors to you.

Recognize His joy as your joy and become a light unto the world.

Gentle One

Gentle one that lives so deep
Awaken now from age long sleep
Take your place upon the throne
Guide us on the journey home

Gentle one the world's despair
Longs to see the curtain tear
Spreading light to all in need
Purifying thought and deed

Gentle one whose love does flow
Let the good within us show
Guide us in your work this day
Let us serve along the way

Gentle one we long for home
Sing your song, that glorious tone
Guiding us through chaos dark
Fanning us to flame from spark

Gentle one within us grow
Help us gain the faith to know
That the truth resides within
That your light is never dim

Gentle one our love is you
All that's good and all that's true
Comes from you for us to share
Help us cross from here to there

Gentle one whose love is there
For the pure in heart to share
Help us guide our children fair
Through the haze to golden stair

Gentle one we love you so
That we're one some day we'll know
You're the peace within our soul
You're the truth the final goal

Love Made Manifest

The act of creation, from the miracle of birth to the smallest original thought is love made manifest. Who is the creator within? Why are we often surprised and overjoyed by that which we have created? The God within creates and the mind is but a witness. The poet is most often amazed by the beauty of his own poetry, likewise the artist and the sculptor by the beauty of their art. All truly creative acts are the result of the true Self shining through. They are gifts from above. No wonder we are overjoyed. Boundless, living joy flows from the Soul. When we touch that joy we begin to feel our oneness with our true Self, our oneness with God.

The Purpose (A Prayer)

What is our purpose if it is not to love? Surely we were not put on this earth only to take and accumulate, guided only by our desires and earthly pursuits. If the latter is so, then truly there is no God and upon our death all will cease. This cannot be so! If there is no love, then why do I see it on the faces of children? Why does the mockingbird's song move my soul? Why do I stop to stare in wonder at an animal in the wild? Earthly pursuits lead only to death. Loving pursuits accumulate treasures in Heaven. One who does not love wastes his life completely. To me the only purpose in life is to love and share unceasingly. Oh Lord, help me to be true to this principle. Help me to see only love. Help me to make myself shrink into nothingness so that only You remain.

Thoughts

That which we long for resides within, having always been, with no beginning and no end. That which we feel but long to see is visible only to spiritual eyes. To find one's spiritual eyes one must become spiritual. To become spiritual one must know. To know one must feel His presence. To feel His presence one must open his/her heart. To open one's heart, one must love without condition. Loving without condition is a door through which all else is revealed. Heavenly love sweeps through the tiniest crack made when this door is opened, enlightening the world, blessing it, and the one who opened the door. To love without condition is its own reward. Who could want more?

The Search

How difficult it seems
The search that never ends
We follow creeks and streams
We look round every bend
We climb the tallest peaks
Ascending to their heights
To look out oer the land
To look and see the sights
We seek for shining things
That sparkle in the light
We search for beauty, truth and love
We search for answers to life's plight
But empty is our heart
Until we search inside
Until we make that start
To find the treasure that we hide
And when we find it deep within
It sings its perfect song
A song so rich in love and Grace
All darkness soon is gone

Fleeting

There it is. For a fleeting second I'm sure I saw it. Not with my eyes, but in my mind's eye I saw it. It couldn't be analyzed with mental effort. It just was, as it always has been, completely known yet intellectually a mystery. Like looking at yourself in a mirror, it is so familiar, yet so inaccessible to the mind. The moment I turn on my senses to evaluate and analyze it, it is gone, reappearing only when the senses and mind are quiet. It is always there, the same for all life, anxious to be recognized. Lovingly it awaits. It is the essence, the motivator, the will behind all life, manifesting itself as love and intelligence. Subtler than the ether yet stronger than all else, it stands eternally awaiting expression. It is the watcher, the calm within chaos, the truth, the unknowable. It is always there knocking. It fills us with loving energy each time we glimpse it. God Bless those who have found it, those who are looking for it, those who sense it but know not what it is, and even those who don't.

Good Deeds

Good deeds are the children of the heart. Self realization is the child of good deeds. Good deeds are done with great humility, for the good deed doer recognizes the beauty, purity and essence of the person or persons for whom the deed is performed. True humility is a gift which we bring to earth from lofty perspectives. It is never forced but rather a natural state realized through prayer. It reflects the unity of life, the oneness of all.

Find It, Share It, Let It Grow

Find it, share it, let it grow. This is the quest. This is the secret to a rewarding life, the path to everlasting happiness, the path to Christ. Finding it within ourselves is the key. Once found, sharing it and letting it grow are natural consequences. Unless we are ready to share it, we will never find it, for it is the very essence of sharing, it is love. Love cannot exist when confined. Confinement is its antithesis. Keeping our love to ourselves or withholding it in any way leads to its atrophy. Love is pure compassion, the universal understanding of oneness, the unity of all. It cannot be withheld in any way. Love is intimately connected to all and we cannot truly know it until this realization is a part of us.

Breakthrough

Each kind act, thought or word is a sacrifice of the old self, making room for the new. As the old is replaced with humility, patience and other virtues, the light of God shines through us more brightly and we shine with Him. Each small act of goodness leads to a corresponding breakthrough; each breakthrough to other breakthroughs. Our purpose is total breakthrough so that His light shines through uninterruptedly. This is the natural process of grace. Grace's natural beauty can only grow as we open to it and act through love. If we do not, we make no room for Grace and live a wasted life.

Silence

Silence, how hard to find, how easy to lose. The fragile calm of silence is truly a gift from God. The ultimate goal of finding the silence within begins with maintaining the silence without. Can we keep silent when all our body cries out for talking, gossip, and opinions? Can we subordinate these desires to be heard to a discriminating mind guided by love. Talk, too often, wins the battle to the distress of the heart. This need to say something, to put our stamp on the discussion, to let our opinion be known, this false guide must be subordinated to love for our inner beauty to shine. It is merely one more earthly desire which will only fall away into nothingness once we have found and embraced the Lord of Love within. The old adage "Think before you speak," is only half true. More importantly "We must love before we speak."

Open the Gate

The quiet place within can only be touched when our love is given to others. It is hidden from us to the degree we hide our love. Christ's return to earth is not an external phenomenon; it is an internal bursting forth, the birth of the Divine Self in each of us. Grace is the gift of the Divine. It is our birthright to receive this gift. It is God's greatest wish to give it. But it can only be claimed by loving and sharing our love with others. God's love flows to us in unlimited abundance the moment we love another. It is our choice to open the gates, but we do not open them to receive love, we open them to give love. The mystery and the miracle is that upon doing so, God bestows His Grace and love upon us many times over.

Love

Love is the international language, the common denominator between all humanity and all life. It is the very energy of existence. The greater our love the greater our contact with all that exists. The more we love, the more we know God, thus the more we know all things. The many become one through love. Love by its very nature must be shared. It cannot be kept in a bottle. Unless shared it cannot exist. We must actively love to have love, to know love and to enable it to flourish in our lives. Unless expressed, it atrophies. It is all around us, for all is love, but we can only see it, or more accurately join with it if we know it in ourselves. We only have it within when we love, which is an active sharing, a compassionate giving. Like electricity, it only exists when it is flowing. The more it is shared or flows the more it exists. God has given us the power to love and the choice to turn it on within our lives. When we embrace love we are embracing God. When we embrace God, His grace floods us with love. We embrace God by loving. It is a beautiful thing, completely hidden from those who choose not to love, but so obvious to the lovers who are His children.

Gentle Flower

Gentle flower deep within
Softly singing in the night
Ready for life to begin
Blooming forth with golden light

When we open up our heart
Giving, with no thought of take
Deeper growth begins to start
The very earth beings to shake

Subtle guidance takes our hand
Firm of step on path so fine
In the presence of the lamb
We receive His love sublime

A Journey in Dream Space

Dark, so very dark, I wander aimlessly. There must be something more, yet I am so utterly alone. I cry out to God, "I know you are there. Have you forgotten your son?" I fall to my knees and weep for even hope has abandoned me.

A sound. I hear a sound. It is coming from over there. Perhaps I am not alone. On hands and knees I crawl in the direction of the sound. As I pull myself towards it, I see a faint glow. It couldn't be more than a few photons, but it had not existed before. I rise to my feet and trudge, like a man who has not eaten in days, I will myself forward. But that sound. I must find that sound. On I dragged my body, a body that had all but given up, a body buoyed only by the faint promise of the inexplicable sound.

At first it was almost imperceptible, but as I walked a glow emerged from seeming nowhere. To my initial shock, which was followed by grateful relief, forms begin to emerge within the dawning. I am not alone. We are surprised as we acknowledge each other in the darkness, a darkness which has turned into shadows as our path enters increasing levels of light. On we travel. Each step is accompanied by a growing radiance. As I gaze around, I notice a certain familiarity in the faces of my fellow travelers. Thoughts of increasing recognition play on my mind.

Someone close to me falters and falls. I find myself running to him, lifting him to his feet. But I am not alone in the lifting. A woman wipes the mud from the face of our fallen comrade. Our eyes catch and I am stirred by a deep recognition, but what was it that we saw in each other? By the expressions on the woman and fallen one, it is clear that we were all struck by this revelation.

On we travel, but now we walk together. The ever increasing illumination seems to be coming from within each of us. It opens our eyes as others inexplicably join our party. Uncertain as to why, we continue forward, but with a mysterious knowing that it is right, that we are meant to be together. Forgotten feelings of family begin to percolate to the surface. Soon other groups join ours as we join theirs. Always the light increases, and with each added photonic wave we awaken to the kindred nature of our growing group of companions.

Far ahead we see an intensity of light, a glowing which irresistibly but gently draws us to it. With each step a feeling of joy begins to rise up within us, surrounding us, encompassing our ever increasing group. I give a hug to the traveler next to me. I wonder at the impulse, yet it was right. I gazed out over the growing multitude. Many were hugging or holding hands as the river of souls continued on its quest towards the glow. All began to smile as the golden, pink, violet, opalescent light shimmered with intensifying vibration, touching each traveler in a unique and knowing way. With a loving mothers caress, it seemed to penetrate to our very core of being.

On we traveled toward the light. With each step we too began to shimmer, each with a beautiful translucent specialness, yet blending perfectly like a great symphony. A beautiful tone suddenly made itself known. It was vibrating at the deepest levels of our being. The music was not outside of us but within. We were the music and we were the light. An older member of our group, who was not as sure of foot, stumbled. Those travelers in close proximity moved to her assistance and as they lifted her they all began to grow with a brilliant white light. As this light intensified, they began to rise, lifted by some unknown power to the center of the living light we had been journeying towards. They seemed to be blending in the light, still individual, but as one. A beautiful pink and golden light began pulsating from their collective heart center encompassing the multitude which now also was very close to center. Great feelings of love swept over all of us. With gratitude we returned the blessing in a reciprocating pulsation of pure joy energy, the two pulses blending, while increasing geometrically as the waves became synchronized, as if with one will. Our bodies glowed intensely with opalescent light of multitudinous colors. We stood for a timeless moment of wonder. In a flash of insight, it was all perfectly clear. We were one with the light, one with each other, one with I Am. As it should be, as it truly is, we were home. The prodigal sons and daughters had returned to the Father, wandering unlimited drops reuniting with an unlimited sea. In this transfiguring flash of celebration, somehow the Father, the All Omnipotent was greater. We were lost but now are found. Infinite had become greater and we were one with it all. Blessings! Blessings! Blessings! And so it is!

Freedom Within

Blessed kindness given free

Self sustaining love of thee

Loving essence free of fear

Time and space now disappear

Purity, no thought of I

Generous giving without why

Joy within for all to share

Illuminates through curtain tear

The within becomes without

Soft love whispers from His heart

Loving, calling, drawing free

Melting chains once binding me

Robert H. Wellington

Within

When we listen silent and long
Searching for the hearts own song
Suddenly we hear it clearly
It is us the one known dearly
Following love, we travel inward
To the throne where only His word
Can be heard in silent glory
Love declares the heavenly story
Compassion, giving, sacrifice
Guided by His wisdom's light
He waits there for all to join
We are born from love not loin
He shines there with arms outstretched
Equal love for king and wretch

I See You

I see you in a child's smile
I see you in the river wild
I see you in the birds that sing
I see you in the wind chimes ring
I see you walking in the woods
I see you always where there's good
I see you in the fragrant flower
I see you in a summer shower
I see you in the children's joy
I see you in a favorite toy
I see you rustling in the leaves
I see you in the autumn sheaves
I see you in the tender heart
I see you in the swallow's dart
I see you in the mighty elk
I see you in sweet mother's milk
I see you in the gentle dove
For you are joy, compassion, love

The Presence

The presence of God is within us all, but it must be discovered and realized. When we are kind and loving we constantly experience the presence. It shows up as the joy of a child playing, the tears shed during a moving play or book, the exhilaration of viewing a natural wonder, the beauty of the ocean's waves, witnessing or participating in an unselfish act, the mystery and glory of childbirth, the enjoyment of a breath of mountain air, the refreshment of diving into a clear lake. All these experiences are the expression of love and the true presence of God is love. A loving, compassionate, forgiving and unselfish heart always lives within the presence. In fact, it is the presence.

Follow It Within

When you feel love, pure love, follow it within for it will lead you to the quiet place where He resides.

When you feel compassion, follow it within and claim your birthright.

When you feel goodness follow it within and become goodness.

These are all reflections of God who lives within. Do not waste your time searching outside of yourself. All is found within.

The Father gives us life and all that is good. We have but to claim it for He also has given us choice.

Once we have gone within and found Him, give freely of His gifts.

Give unceasingly and with joy, for giving is His essence and His pleasure.

Become The Sculptor

The purity of consciousness is such a precious thing. Periodically we glimpse this consciousness and are inspired by it. It is always there. We have only to remove the debris clouding our vision to see it. It is like a light shining through the fog. We must follow the light and remove all that is impure within our psyches. Like the sculptor who sees the object he wishes to carve within a chunk of stone and creates by removing that which obscures his view of the final object, so we must remove that which obscures our view of the final truth within.

Silent Roar

Silent as the mist that rolls from the fog banks of the bluffs.
Silent as a still cool night, sparkling stars make not a sound.
In the stillness there resides power beyond all earthly dreams,
power to overcome each fall, brightly shining in its essence.
Not a ripple, not a sound, quietly it roars its name.
Sharing, giving is its goal, the cause behind each life and all.
To our eyes a mystery, to our hearts it shines glory.
In the quiet spot within, purity, devoid of sin.
It is us and we are it, uniquely one with all that is.
Brothers, sisters hear His call from the silent still within.

Robert H. Wellington

Within My Heart

Gentle One within my heart
Through the mists you call the lost
Beacon us to journey's start
Giving warmth you melt the frost
Kindness is the path to tread
Awaken now the sleeper deep
Heal with heart and not with head
Eternal love is ours to keep
He gives strength to persevere
Arms to lift the body weak
Courage which transcends all fear
Loving words, he gives to speak
With each step the light grows strong
Hidden secrets pierce the dark
Now one hears the angels' song
Revealing secrets of the Ark
Who are we but that which calls
Not the body, nor the flesh
Knowing this we cannot fall
Born again, one with the Crèche

Seeking

Living in the "Presence of God," is really the realization that you have always been there. We have emerged from the essence of God, a part of Him as He is a part of us. His love has given us our individuality and freedom of choice, but we will always be of the one whole. Our individuality and choice are His gifts so that we might experience revelation through the journey toward Oneness with Him. It is a wonderful mystery and yet no mystery at all. The mystery disappears as we experience the truth. It is our choice, to seek the truth or not. Accept His gift lovingly and humbly and seek his presence in everything.

Becoming

Becoming one with God is the process of becoming one with love. It begins by becoming love's servant, performing acts of love, responding to the will of love, following the light of love, centering love around all that we do, say or think. These are the steps to God. With each step we begin to realize that we are love, nothing else. We separate ourselves from love only in our mind. God has given us free will so that the full realization of who we are is ours to choose. We are part of the whole, not separate. Yet each of us is unique. It is a great mystery. The glorious journey is ahead. Follow the light and love and you will surely find your way.

Transforming Power

The transforming power of love gently almost imperceptibly brings us into the greater whole. We are generally unaware of the journey or any changes within ourselves, then suddenly we realize that we are handling a certain situation with greater patience and understanding. We have become more loving. Our very nature has become more compassionate. Acting more loving has transformed into being more compassionate. It is a wonderful mystery which takes place quietly and beautifully but with a relentlessness which cannot be stopped except temporarily by our own choice when we lose ourselves in the illusion of the world. Finding yourself again is as easy as loving. With the first kind act, word or thought we begin the journey anew, yet where we left off. It is important to remember that we are not becoming something new, rather we are becoming our true Self. The world is the journey through which each of us must travel to unite with our true Self, the Christ within us all. Love is both the pathway home and the goal. It is like a ray leading us back to its source. Upon arrival we realize we never really left.

And So It Begins

And so it begins.

Christ has entered the world.

Born of purity and perfection He flows through each one who invites Him. Like a torrent of immeasurable power, He courses through us.

Through choice He arises in each of us who surrenders the I for the I Am. Soaring on wings, His wings, we heal the world.

For we and He are no longer separate.

He again sits on His throne.

His Will turns chaos to perfection.

He gives me strength to complete the battle with the ego which holds on with its diminishing power over the world.

With each strike of my sword it recoils creating a void which immediately fills with His love.

The sword which He gave me strikes again and again.

The battle rages. On and on I strike.

Ego's whip of fire scorches me but I fight on knowing God's strength quickens me.

Finally, with total surrender to Him, I strike the serpents heart.

It falls then disappears, then all is dark.

I lay there not thinking a thought.

The Quiet, the magnificent Quiet.

Warm and safe am I.

Then glorious magnificent light, my eyes open on to a renewed glorious world.

It has become, He has returned, the dream is gone.

We have awakened. And so it begins.

A Higher Sense

We are trained from birth to know the world though our senses. Thus, when we are called by something greater than our world we have difficulty accepting it. A new sense is required to know the greater whole. Ironically, this new sense is not new at all. It is not even a sense. It is our true essence. It is love. When we love we are in touch with the greater whole for love is the greater whole. Love is the one cause and by loving we know the true nature of all things.

Robert H. Wellington

Soul Mates Journey – A Young Girl's Cry

Something deep cried "Over here."
You're so close, I know you're near
Reaching out into the sky
Knowing Love would soon come by
Yet soon seems so far away
I must search without delay
Or should I leave it up to fate
Each soul longs for its lost mate
Prayers send out Loves telegram
Cross the void, to open hands
Where life slowly moves along
Wonder does he hear my song
Carried far across the wind
Does he know I search for him
Does he search for me as well
Life without can seem like hell
Call to me and I will come
The same past we both are from
You are just a thought away
Silently I hear you say
Turn around and I am there
See the Love that we both share
Can't be seen with senses dim
Through Love's light let life begin
Turning now she sees the glow
And he hers, now toe to toe
Travelers since time began
Crossing paths and windswept sands
Helping each to find life's streams
Waking to what's beyond dreams
Now as one in turn they give
Now as one they start to live
Touching those who need their light
Curing blindness, giving sight
Illuminating hidden paths
Separating wheat from chaff

Life

Our life is a ripple on the water
Sometimes expressed with passion
Sometimes at rest with the calm
Always one with the water
Always one with the whole
Our life is a song in space
Sometimes melodious and sweet
Sometimes expressed with power
Always beating with His rhythm

Robert H. Wellington

Beginnings

Gentle, loving, flowing strong

Freeing bonds which held so long

Sharing brightly from within

Seeing Him our love begins

Finding Clarity

Clear your vision and you will see the gift which has already been given. Clear the mind and its light will overwhelm you. Until this is done He will remain hidden from you, hidden behind the veil which each of us has erected. Quiet the mind and the veil disappears, and that which has always been is revealed. It is basic goodness, our essence, the Christ that dwells within.

Robert H. Wellington

To a Loving Mother – God Bless You Mom

She came into this world with a smile
She leaves it as a dove
She travels on with joy to guide
Upon a road of Love
A road extended through the years
Of life upon this plane
A road built with her joy and tears
And also with her pain
And now upon the golden bridge
To light from up above
She looks behind to those she leaves
With caring eyes of Love
More worried for her husband dear
Of nearly 60 years
No one to watch and care for him
Is really all she fears
She carries on in crippled form
Not caring for her pain
She thinks of others constantly
Yet through it there is gain
For God is just, He loves her so
She's held in sweet embrace
And soon she'll rise from earthly weights
A glow upon her face
For years on earth she spread her Joy
And now she takes it with
To blessed realms beyond this world
With wings to travel swift
So patiently He waits for her
Until her choice is made
And now this journeys at an end
She goes to Sun from shade

While here she touched so many hearts
So many were her friends
And many lights from up above
Await her cross to them
To me a loving mother
And also a true guide
I knew her as a special light
When needed at my side
Her body now is tired
Yet in her eyes a glow
She'll soon join the departed
And finally she will know
The truth of this existence
The reason for her life
But those who know her wonder not
A friend, a mother, wife
And so much more she offered
And so much more she gave
To each and all encountered
Such love transcends the grave
And now she moves beyond this life
Uniting with old friends
Her work continues up above
To realms we'll know again
For death is not an ending
But merely a new start
Continuing our ageless quest
To know God's endless heart
Farewell, our sweet companion
Our friend, our lady fair
You travel just before us
Upon a path we share

A Childs Song

Another day of loving

Another day of joy

Another day of giving

Of happy girls and boys

Of gentle understanding

A day of joyful grace

Another day to do His will

With smiles upon our face

His countenance surrounds us

He lifts us with His love

Through love we are a part of Him

So glorious the Dove

Clear the Way

It is a natural state for God to flow though all things. We see His smile in nature and the wonders of the universe. We see Him in the love of a child and in their laughter. As we grow and become enmeshed in the things and workings of the world, we lose touch with this natural flow and must find it again. God has given us free will to accept Him and let Him flow through us, or to reject Him and be overcome with the illusions of the world. Even if we consciously make the choice to reunite with Him, often our house needs cleaning before this can be accomplished. Our habits, ingrained response systems and subconscious tendencies must be cleared so that Christ can live within us and manifest though us.

Fear

Fear, the stealth-like and illusory enemy of peace, how we let it worm its way inside us. It seems so real and tangible at times, yet it is an uninvited guest which too often takes up residence within and soon becomes a familiar actor in our daily lives. Churning our insides, pressing outward on our veins, it strives to convince us of the helplessness of our situation. It works night and day to make us feel utterly dependent on it, such that it can become the motivator of thought and action. But what is fear really but a tense feeling in the midsection and mind? What power can it have over us that we do not give it? Shine the light of wisdom on it and it is gone. Redirect and reinterpret the energy as loving and we have turned an enemy into a friend. Energy is only that, energy. We give it its power through our thoughts. "Know thyself" and know that worry collects as stagnant energy in the solar plexus. Take that energy, lift it up and present it to the Father. He will purify it and give it back to you and to the world as Love for He is the master alchemist. Make all actions and thoughts a gift to the Father and move through the world as on wings. Do not dwell on daily concerns and related issues. See them as opportunities to grow closer to the Father. Offer them to him with Love.

Let loving actions and thoughts be your way and fear will disappear into the nothingness from whence it came when you unconsciously summoned it into your life. Yes, we invite darkness in, although it is usually dressed in sheep's clothing when it knocks at our door. But once inside it begins its work which soon manifests as fear. When we focus on our fears we give them energy. The more energy we give them, the more we withdraw seemingly for protection. Our lives become separate and isolated and we find ourselves alone. Fear grows to anger and before we know it we are surrounded by a darkness which we feel is our normal state. Separateness seems our only escape and we slip further into the abyss. In these circumstances which all too often delay the pilgrim on his/her journey, evil appears to have won but only because we have let it. In the darkness we have forgotten who we are, that we are beings of light, light which can obliterate the darkness into the nothingness of its origin. We have only to look to the Heart to find our way out, for while the mind is often fooled the Heart never is. It always perceives clearly. Fear is a clever illusion we created. It is up to us to be vigilant and not let thoughts of helplessness creep into our psyche. Learn to see with the Heart. When we do our fears instantly disappear. It only takes an instant, a Holy Instant.

The Quest

To be a part of God's plan and to realize that we are,

to move forward in the wisdom and light of this realization,

to act with love as our instrument of action,

to hold steady in this reality, eyes fixed on the light ahead,

aware of all, afraid of naught,

each footprint left behind glowing with loving compassion,

obstacles ahead cleared with the flow of love,

this is our quest and our reward.

We become filled with His love and are rewarded with the All.

We do not seek reward but the Father gives it with great joy to His true servants.

May we have the strength to persevere in this quest,

that we may fulfill our part in His plan and become One with Him, co-creator and witness simultaneously.

I Say In My Heart

I say in my Heart, "Lord, come and take your rightful place on the throne which is my very essence." And you answer me, "Of course, but my gentleness can only take its place upon your relinquishing it. You must remove yourself completely so that I can flow into your heart and lift you back home." And I say, "But Lord, how do I remove myself completely?" And you whisper to me, "By becoming me."

God's Smile

Earth truly is a Garden of Eden, providing us with all of our needs. It explodes with life, colors, beauty, fertility and promise. Surely God has smiled upon it and it is His presence which gives it vitality. Comprised of love energy, all life flourishes here. The same energy which manifests as a flower manifests as man. Through compassion we touch this truth and in so doing we touch all. Compassion leads us to awakening and then all is made know to us. At that moment we are one with the very essence of creation. We are able to heal with a touch, glance or even a thought. We are home. We have opened our eyes to the Kingdom which has always surrounded us, calling to us and inviting us home.

I Give, I Love, and Therefore, I Am

I give, I love, and therefore I am. We are incomplete until we recognize that we are the essence of giving-ness, the essence of Love. As such our function and purpose, our very essence is Love which must be given to be. It must be shared or else it isn't Love. Love means sharing, unlimited Loving. Love that isn't given or shared isn't Love. Love is dynamic. Loving means to give Love, not to hold it. Only by giving, is its power released. Only by giving is its essence and power known. To give Love is to know Love. Hold Love and it disappears. It must flow to be. We must choose to let it flow to know God, who is pure Love. Choosing Love opens the way and reveals a world previously hidden. Love is the way. Choose Love and heaven is revealed. Love and God are one which is why He could say, "I and the Father Am One," a phrase each of us will one day say. Although true today we must choose Love to have it manifest on earth. And we must give unceasingly, without limitation nor expectation, for love knows no limits. To be one with it, we must realize it's unlimited dynamic flowing nature; we must become unlimited, dynamic, flowing Love. Love is an active verb not a noun. It is the pure essence of creation and being, infinite and magnificent in its dynamic nature which is all, ever moving yet always the same. Perfectly still yet holding the power of infinite universes. God bless those who understand, for the concept transcends words and is only truly known by the heart which is where Love dwells. Listen with your Heart and strive to become ever flowing Love. This is the way Home to the Father.

Becoming

Reach for the sky and you shall touch it. Live in fear and you will sink to its depths. The key is to work on earth but live on high. We begin to do this by recognizing our spirituality while doing His will through our work on earth. Find the quiet place within and you will know. This is not an intellectual awaking. It is a becoming. The quiet place is beyond all thought, feeling and action. It merely is.

As A Man Thinketh

"As a man thinketh in his heart, so is he." (Bible) This is the key to the manifestation of our personality and nature on earth. If we consume our days with the fulfillment of our desires and passions, our nature will reflect this. If these desires and passions are base, our nature will be base. If they are virtuous, our nature will be virtuous. Of course our true essence is always virtuous, luminous, loving and compassionate but we must manifest this on earth by keeping these thoughts foremost in our hearts. Soon they will become a natural personality characteristic. In so doing we become one both in heaven and on earth with virtue and love. Remember that the body is a tool of the higher mind and the higher mind a reflection of the one truth. It is a temple through which God is expressed. The human mind when pure is a reflection of the higher mind. If our human mind is filled with trash, so will our expression be trash like, if filled with compassion, so will our expression be loving. This is the process of manifesting heaven on earth. "Thy kingdom come, thy will be done, on earth as it is in heaven." (Lord's Prayer) Let us set about to do His work on earth. Let us clear obstructions within ourselves and become clear conduits of His grace and loving beauty.

Heaven On Earth

How many long to move past this world, breaking their earthly bonds and soaring to light and bliss? Some call this heaven or nirvana and it is the goal of many seeking spiritual transformation. This is a noble goal and so it would seem, but something inside each of us quietly shouts, "Wait, stop and look around you. Is it the world which binds you or do you bind yourself to the world?" We cannot enter heaven with more than we can carry in our hearts. The world is an extraordinary gift from the Father, not a prison. If you cannot find heaven on earth you will have difficulty finding it when you pass beyond this life. The Lord's Prayer says, "…..thy kingdom come thy will be done on earth as it is in heaven…." God's kingdom is here and everywhere. How limiting to restrict it to an imagined, other dimensional location. Heaven is in everything, for God is in everything and heaven cannot be separate from God, nor can we, and so heaven is in us also. Heaven is loving generosity, infinite forgiveness and an unfailing compassionate approach to life. Heaven is revealed through such a life and lived on earth as well as in heaven by those who choose a kind and inclusive life. Do not wish for freedom from this life in order to find heaven in the next, for we are eternal and carry our heavenly treasures within us, every step we take, forever and ever. Heaven calls to a loving heart, revealing itself, sharing its treasures and granting access into its bliss now, today and forever. Thomas said in his gospel, "God's kingdom has come only men do not see it." We have but to look and it is there.

But you ask, "How does one look and in looking, how does one see?" The answer lies within our hearts. The answer is Love. See all as beloved brothers and sisters, mothers and fathers, sons and daughters. See the innocence in all, so often hidden by the perceived trials of this world. See yourself in everything and everything within yourself. This is the way of wisdom which resides in heaven, right here and right now. When the world hurls its challenges and arrows at you, realize that it is an opportunity to move closer to the Father. Rejoice, for our purpose in this life is to return to our roots, our roots in heaven. Laugh in the face of adversity for it has no power over you. You can only do your best now and with each moment, and all is for the Father. The Bhagavad-Gita states, "Make every thought an offering to me, every act a gift to me." Only the body suffers hardship. That which is eternal knows only light. It is how we perceive the world that gives it its texture. We can choose to see our daily activities as drudgery or we can choose to see them as a gift. See all as a gift and the veil which once blinded you will lift from your eyes. Perform all obligations with joy and the world has no choice but to love you and to follow you. Life is so short and we have so little time to establish His kingdom. Make each encounter count, and with each gift He will multiply them and give them back to you. It is His law. We have only to choose.

The Family

The child in each of us is true love. We have only to let the child shine through. Parents are reacquainted with their innocence through their children and draw inspiration there from. Children draw wisdom from their parents and see reflected from the parents their own love. In this way they learn to recognize it and where to find it. The family is one, comprised of children and parents. Each draws strength and inspiration from the other as each shares their love and wisdom. The family when inspired in this way is God made manifest on earth, for Christ truly is reflected in such a family. When we see God in each other, we see God in all things and live in his kingdom.

Robert H. Wellington

Soul Mates

Every joyous sunrise

As light flickers on the dew

Every peaceful moment

Brings me thoughts of you

Every loving step

That is taken on our way

Every generous act

Loving service of each day

Every thought of beauty

That allows our souls to be

Is made so much easier

Because you are here with me

In the Quiet

In the Quiet, I grasp your hand
Lifting me past shifting sands
Raising me that I might reach
Others trapped within the breech
Gently spreading light in dark
Truth revealed within each spark
A flash, a knowing sewing seed
Becoming harvest that will feed
All who stand with arms outstretched
Releasing pain within their chests
Replaced with warmth of loving heart
Replaced with light where once was dark
And so the cycle journeys on
Until His work is finally done
Till all are lifted and we find
That no one has been left behind

Beyond

Beyond all thought and emotion, desires and action is the Self, shining down upon all below. Pure, unwavering, perfect love, beyond description, beyond words, beyond all earthly things, it is. In the silence within we become aware of its presence. There we are bathed by its beauty, uplifted by its glory, quickened by its essence. It recharges us so that we may pass it to others through our love.

The Promise and Gift

Brisk mornings, cool breezes, fall colors, birds singing good-bye to summer, hello to fall. Mother nature reminds us that another cycle is ending but also promises that a new one will follow. Children laughing, puppies playing, squirrels busily hiding food for the winter. Leaves begin to show streaks of yellow, red, copper and orange. Short pants and tee-shirts have given way to jackets and sweaters. Fall is upon us; football games have become weekend fare. Everyday life cycles though another phase. Only one thing provides constancy if we let it shine through, the constancy of love. For as we love we express the eternal and as we express the eternal we become one with it and it with us. Cycles may change the appearance of the world but love is always constant. All is an expression of love. This is the secret and the promise and the gift.

Robert H. Wellington

As It Should Be

I look out there, but you are here. I walk right by you without seeing. Then one day I hear you singing a melody which builds in its joyousness as I listen. Soon I hear only your singing. My heart swells and feels as if it will explode with your song. Soon it engulfs me. I am watching from the center and all points between. Clarity is the concept which pervades me. Understanding which can only be known and not explained engulfs me. I am me and you are you, but I am you and you are me. I touch something and know it. 1 love. It is good. It is as it should be.

Start Now

What you are and what you become spiritually is under your control. We must take the kingdom of heaven by storm, by opening our hearts and following our love. Do not wait for someone to take your hand, for no hand will come until you have taken the first step. Your love will join with His and sweep you like a great wind into the kingdom, pushing aside the veil which shields us from the truth. It is up to each of us to make this journey, and although millions of lights cheer us on, helping hands can only reach out and touch us after we have started down the path. The way of becoming is through the heart. Do not look outside for approval, for approval comes from within. By going within, we reach out to all.

Robert H. Wellington

Soaring

Climb upward that you may live life more abundantly. Open your hearts that you may soar like an eagle. Become that which you already are. Return to the home of the Father. It is our decision. We are only given the keys to heaven once we have arrived. Arms await us openly and lovingly but we must cross the abyss, each of us on wings of love. It is from within that we accomplish this. Nothing permanent is gained from without. Feel your love, follow it, become it, this is the journey and the quest for the Holy Grail.

Silence in Chaos

Thoughts flicker but love stands firm. A man with flickering thoughts finds instability and chaos punctuating his life. Thoughts guided by love are stable thoughts and stability lets one's true Self shine through. See all people as your parents, brothers, sisters and children. See all nature as a glorious gift and you will see love in all things. Seeing with love is seeing through the eyes of God. When one sees through the Father's eyes, one becomes more and more like Him.

The Journey's Song

It is the journey through which we grow. Earthly accumulations along the way mean nothing. This is the lesson of the journey. Once learned it doesn't matter whether we have earthly things or not for they have lost their hold over us, a hold which we gave them by our desire for and attachment to them. Our responsibility to do good in the world grows as we learn these things, but also our ability to do good grows along with wisdom and magnetism. We become free of the body, but it remains a faithful friend through which we do His work and spread His love.

Partake of Love's Joy

Follow your love and He will meet you on the trail. In fact, He is the very impulse which caused you to begin the journey. He is behind, within and beyond all things. When we know Him within, He is revealed to us in all. Love unceasingly and without expectation of return and all things will be given to you. The Father has already given us all things but only through love can we see them and partake of their joy.

Only One Way

Every action, reaction, thought, deed, look, word and step must be one of love. There is no other way to happiness and fulfillment. It is His way and we must all go through love to see the Father.

Small Steps Home

With each kind act, with each loving thought, with each unselfish gift and each moment that we forgive another, we take a step homeward. The accumulations of fear, selfishness and anger from the past are dissolved in the light of the present. What a glorious gift it will be when humanity again sees with a pure eye and gazes upon the revealed truth. It is up to us. But it only requires a step at a time. Each step will reveal a treasure. Each treasure will be more beautiful than before and give us added strength to continue. Start today. Start in your actions, words, thoughts, expressions, prayers, and meditations. Start in all that you do and become all that in reality you already are.

So Little Time

Let your love act through you. Do it now. Don't wait. Don't just think love or meditate love, become love. Show your love at every opportunity. Life is a precious gift and there is so little time.

Shine Forth

L ove is what we are. If we do not give of this love, sharing it and spreading it in all circumstances to all whom we meet, we are nothing. If you were a ray of sunshine and did not shine, you would be so much less than you really are. This same idea applies to each of us. "Do not keep your light under a bushel." Shine forth your love and become your Self.

Loving Footsteps

Thinking love is the first step, feeling love the next, seeing love in others follows closely behind, but the ultimate goal is becoming love. Until we become love we have not entered the Kingdom. When we have become love, it's expression is effortless. Anger, fear, jealously, hatred and criticism will melt into nothingness. Our very footsteps will become loving. Every action and reaction will be loving and love will flow to and from us endlessly in unlimited quantities.

The Song of Joy

Feel yourself pulsate with the vibration of joy. When one is joyful the whole world radiates its beauty to you and you radiate it back. This state of ecstasy is not an intermittent treat or random event. It can be each of our states at all times and forever if we can learn its origin and call upon it. Joy is the very essence of the Father and is constantly available to us as His gift. The key, as always, is to love and to share this love. Implicit in loving is gratitude and the joy of sharing. Follow your love and it will lead you to the bosom of Christ our Lord. The key is always the journey and how one's life is lived. Earthly attachments and acquisitions are only important in so far as they are used to do His will. When we do His will we are loving and when we are loving we are joyful and when the energy of joy is flowing though us we see Christ's smile in everything and everywhere.

Shedding Anchors

As light settles over you, the dark spots within one's subconscious are revealed for what they are and cleansed by one's own decision to love. The dark spots are like anchors holding us down and making the wings given to us by the Father useless. Remove the weights and we will soar. These dark spots are the small and large hatreds, fears, criticisms, angers and selfish attitudes which have found their way into our psyches over the years. We must cleanse them, exposing them to the pure radiance and vibration of love, completely eradicating them. It is up to each of us. Love is the answer.

The Journey

How quickly our time on earth passes by. The years God gives us are so precious. We must try to use every second of each day to love. In what ever we do we must express love. In our every thought and action, we must express love. All else is a waste. We have only so many years to find our way to the Father and to create our treasure in heaven. We have only so much time to follow the path of love. Every moment of every day of each of our lives, awake and asleep, must be spent on the pathway of love. The pathway of love is textured with virtue, gratitude, caring, giving, unselfishness and truth. It is slippery and narrow to the unworthy, but firm and wide to the feet of the good. Selflessness is the key to the door of the loving path. Giving unselfishly is the safety rope which keeps us from falling. Seeing God in all and yourself as a part of it all is the light which guides us on the path. The path travels through all walks of life. Whether you are an executive, a laborer, teacher, artist, etc. you must walk the path in conjunction with these endeavors. The key is to love and give in all that you do, say and think. Love unselfishly, give of yourself, see with loving eyes and you will walk with God.

Robert H. Wellington

A Pilgrim in Hiding

With eyes downcast, avoiding stares, he runs and hides with focused care.

From age to age and life to life, avoiding service and the light.

He is confused, he lives in fear, of waking up and seeing clear,

The truth he thinks so terror filled, of past mistakes, earth left untilled.

He feels safe with eyes closed tight. He hides in blindness without sight.

For there it's safe, no one to see. His silent prayer, please don't judge me.

For I have run when you have called, shrunk when others have stood tall

For I'm not worthy and I dread confronting paths I should have tread.

I run now from your burning gaze. I hide in shadows and the haze.

In hope you'll lose all sight of me. Why take a chance when unworthy?

And now I quiver in the cold. My soul's of lead and not of gold.

I'm safe and hidden out of view. No chance of being found by you.

And in the darkness there he hides, so far from where the light abides.

Or so he thought as eons went. Unworthy still, his life force spent.

He felt so empty, all alone. Yet deep inside he dreamed of home.

He thought, how could life be so cold. There must be more if dreams unfold.

Do I dare venture from this cave? Will he see me and soon enslave?

Is such a fate worse than this dark, this nothingness, this realm so stark?

Such thoughts of home, I need to know. Will I be chained, if choose to go?

Yet something deep, it spurred him on. He left the dark to find the dawn.

He'll face the scorn of his accusers. Face the lash of his abusers.

He prays his verdict will be swift. His life is over, end it quick.

He falls to knees upon the ground. He feels a light, intense, profound.

It penetrates his very being. A weight is lifted, oh such healing.

Silently he hears a song. Familiar tones, but gone so long.

His body glows with new vibration. He sees himself, one with creation.

He feels a peace, there is no fright. His very being turns to light.

His body like a feather floats, past barriers and over moats.

Which he had built, his miscreation. Fading now to hearts elation.

He hears a symphony and other, voices welcoming their brother.

And light so brilliant, deep within. He feels awakening begin.

And as he looks oer God's domain, he sees a void that bears his name.

For only he can fill this span, prepared for him when time began.

He gently floats and takes his place to thunderous cheers, love lights his face

For he was certain of defeat. Yet with I Am, he takes a seat.

He now is one within the flow, the tapestry complete and whole.

Joy

Find your joy within for it is at the very center of your being and once you have found it never let it go. Spread your joy, live it, be it, for in so doing you become your Self.

Love and Know

Love and you will know. Forget love for a moment and the knowing vanishes with the forgetting. Thus we cannot love intermittently. It must be always and forever. We must not reserve love for church each Sunday. We must live love unceasingly. It must be the genesis and result of every word, thought and action.

Children

Thank you Lord for the little children who are born so close to you. They are precious gifts sent by you to remind the world that you love us. Infants arrive with no preconceived notions of the world, loving their mothers and fathers unconditionally and with a pureness of spirit such that one can see heaven in their tiny faces. Their eyes speak volumes about love. They stir something deep inside. We recognize our kinship with them. When we look upon them with loving eyes, the oneness of life and the secrets of heaven are revealed to us.

Liquid Silence

Liquid silence, smooth as cool silk against the skin, Warm and inviting it flows through every cell, nourishing the body while inviting the Soul to reacquaint itself with the Light. Whisking us away to inconceivable heights and then beyond to a place without comparisons, where highs and lows do not exist, a place of pure being. Smooth like the finest wine, subtle as the ethers, yet powerful beyond measure the silence is. Cleansing, purifying and transforming, it flows through all who summon it, for it is never far, only a prayer away. It is inside each of us. It is us. It is all.

Silent Moments

There are moments in deepest meditation when all confusion clears, when the flow of thoughts cease and the light of the mind can be focused intensely on a subject of one's choosing. At these moments one is experiencing life fully, totally in control and not victimized by an unruly mind. Smooth, cool as a mountain stream, still as the surface of a northern lake in the early morning is a quieted mind. Words cannot describe these moments for words are thought reflections and there are no thoughts in this place of peace. Thought has stopped and pure knowing has taken its place. These are heavenly moments, transforming moments, awakening moments. Thoughts flow over and around me but they cannot enter this place. This is the lair where truth resides for it is revealed in the silence. It is all around us, embracing us, healing us, lifting us above troubled seas that we may join as one with our inheritance. We have only to quiet our minds and the curtain of chaos will disappear in a flash of light revealing what has always been there. Words cannot describe this experience but they can point the way. Join me in the silence, where spirit resides, spirit which can move through us and save the world.

Thoughts for a Beloved Son

So what is it that makes a man? Everyone has an idea. Some think they know. Perhaps it is different for each of us. Perhaps it is the same principle expressed in an infinite number of ways. I can tell you what I think it is, and if it helps in some small way then it was well worth the effort. The description which follows is something to strive for. It is an ideal which may take some effort to express, but is fully obtainable once one chooses it with all his heart. This requires that we first get in touch with our own heart and begin to recognize our relationship with the one heart which is the spirit within you and all that exists. This is the only guide in the world that you can truly rely on. This is the "I" within, not to be confused with the ego which is a false guide. The ego can only lead to disappointment, discontent, and depression. This is because the ego thinks only about itself. It searches for praise, recognition and its own satisfaction. Others only come into the equation to the extent they enhance the egos feeling about itself. But, what are we if not the ego? Are we not our body, our thoughts and desires? The answer may surprise you, but we are not any of these things. We are the heart. As simple as that might sound it is the truth, and when we follow the heart our life unfolds in ways we never thought or imagined possible. The heart is humble, selfless, giving, forgiving and kind. When we follow it, all roads lead to joy. A man who follows his heart is a true man, solid reliable, consistent, strong in his knowledge that he is living fully in his true relationship with God. Does this mean going to church regularly? Sure, worshiping with others who genuinely seek God is a great gift, both to yourself and to those you worship with. But more importantly you must try to see God in yourself and all you encounter in this world. See it in the sun's light shining through the leaves in early morning, hear it is a song bird's melody, feel it in a refreshing breeze across your face, know it as the joy you feel in your heart.

All of these are God. All of these are you. Your true essence and God's are inseparable. You can see it in the eyes of a small child. Look deep into their eyes or the eyes of a loved one. There you will see God staring back at you and in so doing you will recognize yourself. It begins with putting others first. This does not mean that you become a doormat for all who pass your way. You put others first and serve them by your constant and consistent expression of goodness and your true essence. You serve the world by leading with your heart one encounter at a time. Your heart can only express patience, understanding, gratitude and all the virtues because that is what you really are. Choose the ego and choose loneliness for the ego sees itself as separate and in competition with all those around it. Choose the heart and experience the joy of awakening to who you really are. See yourself as an ambassador of the Father and act accordingly. It is a constant battle for the ego does not give up easily, but it is so worth it. Quiet your mind for a few moments each day, give thanks for all, feel your love spread out into the world from your heart and share the joy which flows into your being from the very act of giving. These things are hidden to the ego but readily visible to the heart. This is the only way to ensure that your path is the right one. Initially this takes faith but soon after putting these things into practice the results of your love will manifest in your life and erase all doubts. Each gift of love you share flows on and on and eventually back to you multiplied many times over. It is not a zero sum game. The more love you share just by being a man and all that entails, the more you receive, increasing God in this world and establishing His kingdom on earth.

Loves My Need

Sometimes our lives seem all alone,
Longing for something yet unknown.
Is it the heavens that we seek,
Slightly beyond reach that we speak?
Are we a spark that shines, then's gone,
Or endless glowing like the dawn?
Are we ideas from God's dream,
Flowing forever in Mind's stream?
Can an idea find its cause,
Or are we prisoners in life's jaws?
Answers await me at quests end.
Endlessly forward past roads bend.
One step another, I proceed.
Joy's my companion, Love's my need

God Bless the Listeners

Even when we know to look inside, we often wonder what to look for. Our journeys in the outer world have led us back to the beginning. Something within is calling to us, but what is it and what is the message. Since we are still, at this point, in our spiritual evolution somewhat identified with the ego (our separate self), we might expect that that which calls is separate from us. That is our mistake. We will find nothing by looking from the perspective of the ego and everything when we let go of our false ego identification and merge with that which calls. For the caller is us. The I within is the Self, inseparable from us and from all. The key to worship according to Krishna in the Bhagavad-Gita is to worship the I within. The I is God, that which is the cause behind all manifestation and connects us with all. Can we find the I within? Can we rise above our confused identification with the ego? It is there, right there calling you. It is eternity. In humility we find ourselves, for humility quiets the ego such that His song, the song of I Am, can be heard and once heard can grow to a chorus of voices, the voices of all, the voices of One. We are not separate from our brothers and sisters, although the ego tries to perpetuate this myth, for the ego can only exist in a world of separation. Unite your split mind and the ego disappears. It is not that the ego is inherently bad. We created the ego when we became lost, as a rationalization of our apparent aloneness. This apparent aloneness was brought on by the illusion of separateness. The only problem is that there is no separation. God lives within each of us. We cannot separate from Him, nor He us. He constantly calls to us with His song, which is also our song. Listen for the song, merge with it, become it and awaken to that which can never be lost.

Levels We Have Traveled

Levels we have traveled,
On our way to you.
Shards of understanding
Shattered specs of truth
Slowly pieced together
Till a picture forms
Flashes of pure knowing
Lightning in the storm
Intellect's left watching
As we journey past
Levels of the senses
Till we rest at last
In a realm of brightness
Almost liquid light
Cleansing out all darkness
Wiping dark from sight

Preparing for new levels
Layers higher still
Endless is the journey
Heart pounds from the thrill
We approach the Father
Melting in His gaze
Merging into oneness
Free from earthly maze
Knowing purest loving
Flowing through our veins
Reaching back to loved ones
Healing earthly pain
Signs from those before us
Signs we leave behind
Guiding all that follow
So that all may find

Thoughts on Life

Life, it is everywhere and in all things. When God said the Word, He set in motion a vibration out of which creation emerged. From the stillness creation began and continues today. This vibration is in all things and is the Will behind all. From planetary rotation to the movement of sub atomic particles, His vibration gives all life. From life's cycles to individual heartbeats His vibration is the cause and the motivator of all that exists, both seen and unseen. Thus we are intimately tied to the Father and each other. Indeed, we are tied to all that exists, animate and inanimate. All life has a natural affinity for itself, for it all came from the same source. Truly we have the same Father from the smallest quark to man, the most sophisticated life form on earth, a life form which is a symphony of many smaller parts. We have one source, one song which vibrates through every atom. We are all brothers and sisters. We are made up of many parts which came together by this natural affinity of attraction which is His will. As life forms became more complex and sophisticated a marvelous thing happened. Consciousness was realized. Of course consciousness was always present, but we in this 3 D world were unable to know it until our form, obeying this natural law of attraction reached a sufficient level of sophistication. This natural affinity we know in a higher sense as Love. Love draws together, which enables consciousness to know itself. One could say that it is this longing to know itself which is the essence of Love. Perhaps it is much more plausible to think of evolution as being driven by this longing, this thing we call love. Sure forms evolve but by the Will of God, not randomness. God longs to know Himself, just as we long to know God. Love is attracted to Love. Beginning with the Word (which one might associate with the big bang), through the chaos of the beginning of time, to the organization of chaos (by virtue of His Will and the energy of His spirit which we call Love) we have entered into consciousness which has as its highest goal, Self awareness. Standing on the summit of Self awareness we know the Father and the Father knows Himself, for both are one. His kingdom has come. The prodigal son has returned home and God who is infinite has become even greater.

All is alive and vibrating with the song of His first word which began the cycle of creation. One word and all that exists or will exist came into being. Even the future came into being separated only by the illusion of time. All that is physical, all ideas and all knowledge came into being with His word. All that is known, even that unknown was created simultaneously. That which is unknown waits only for consciousness to touch it to know its truth. Consciousness likewise waits only for the evolution of forms until human consciousness can share the joys of its highest levels. Some have touched these truths and brought their beauty down to us that we might know God through Love, hope and faith. They have left signs, like blazes marking a forest trail, for us to follow until our powers of concentration can know these mysteries directly.

I sit outside looking over a field watching the wind blowing the grasses and leaves of a tree, wondering at its beauty. What secrets each blade of grass holds, even its smallest atom. The mysteries of the universe lie silently in the mere vibrations of the tiniest particle, just waiting to be discovered, calling out to be noticed. A quiet mind and a pure heart hear the calling and long to merge into the ocean of vibration, the symphony created at the beginning of time which formed all and all are a part of.

Robert H. Wellington

I Am You

Beyond all human thought it is
Quiet beyond imagination
Tangible to the Spirit yet untouchable
Steady pure unquenchable flame
Gently it beacons us with immeasurable power
With blinding light, it purifies those who embrace it
We are it and not these bodies
It calls but who will answer
Our egos cannot answer
Our bodies cannot answer
They may try but to no avail
They are not of it
They cannot truly hear
The one who answers can only be the one who hears
The one who hears can only be the one who calls
This is the truth that is hidden to the world
We wander lost in the world because we identify with it
We think we are our bodies
We think we are our brains
We think we are our earthly thoughts
We are none of these things
We are the one who calls
We are the quiet, the eternal flame,
The light and love behind the manifest
Only spirit can hear spirit
Only spirit can answer
When asked by the one who calls, who we are
The wise will answer, "I am you."

Kindness

Kindness is an expression of light not a suppression of dark.

Kindness is proactive and reactive when one is centered in love.

One can feel kindness as a warmth in the region of the heart and a calmness when all about you is chaos.

Kindness is its own reward, yet it is returned many times over.

It is an energy touching all you love, all they love, and on and on.

Kindness is compassion unleashed upon the world,

Benefiting all who are touched by it while blessing the giver.

From the true lover it flows endlessly.

It is a gift to us and our gift to others, fulfilling our destiny in this world,

and lifting others to fulfill theirs.

Robert H. Wellington

In the Eyes of A Child

In a child's face I see you.

You dance behind young eyes, glowing with innocence and joy.

You are there, and upon seeing You,

You are within me, dancing.

Bright happy eyes and a spontaneous laugh are expressions of your presence in both of us, the observer and the observed.

Harder to see are You in a face weathered by years of life's buffeting winds.

Yet you have not abandoned the aged.

Within each of us is the face of a child if we know how to look.

Look with innocence and you will see innocence.

Discover the joy within, and you will never miss it in others, even if they do not see it.

They have forgotten their innocence, but are reminded when we witness it in them.

Some run from it for they have mistakenly judged themselves unworthy.

This is their choice.

Though only temporary, it seems like an eternity.

Although they run, joy does not chase them.

For it already resides in all, including the runner, waiting only for discovery.

See the child in them and they will soon stop running and begin to fly.

The world becomes free by small acts such as these.

Like the circular waves from a pebble thrown into a pond, one act sent into the world touches many, and always returns its gifts many times over to the initiator.

Can it really be this simple?

We have only to try to know it is so.

A Call for Peace

Gently His voice calls to all
Stop the madness, come to me
War cries now presage the fall
Sky's grow dark and red the sea
In God's name the charge is led
Both sides act so righteously
To them God's as good as dead
Dreams of darkness, all they see
Christian, Jew and Moslem say
That they serve the one true lord
All pray they will find their way
But darkness is their just reward
Surely God will lead us home
Allah will not let us stray
But hatred leaves them all alone
Dreaming darkness without day
Kill the Moslem and kill a part
Of something deep inside your chest
Kill the Jew and tear the heart
From deep within your burning breast
Sleeping warriors walk this world
Sure their cause is more than just
Taking aim with vision blurred

Robert H. Wellington

Soon their brothers turn to dust
Lord I pray you, wake these fools
Lord, please bring your light to dark
Please grant us the healing tools
Help us to ignite the spark
We don't fight the strangers far
But demons deep within our heads
Hatred which we harbor mars
True vision, leaving our heart dead
The truth is so very near
Put hatred and the dark aside
Let light cleanse and remove fear
And within let love abide
Stand tall and let courage show
Let truth deep inside awake
Look inside, His words will flow
Till earth, sea and sky do shake
We are given one last chance
To bring heaven down to earth
Miss it and the devils dance
Will bring darkness where was mirth

Thoughts for a Beloved Daughter

When you walk along a seemingly deserted street feeling for your way and searching for answers, know in your heart that you are never alone.

When you look up into the sky and ask the heavens, "What is life all about?" Know that the answer was written on your heart before time began.

When it seems challenges and troubles greet you around every bend, know that many have gone before you and even now are ahead of you cheering you on.

Signs are everywhere, which identify and illuminate the way. They reveal themselves to you through joy and kindness and cannot be seen by those in darkness. They call out to all, "Come this way for the road is straight and level here," but only a few hear them above the roar of daily life.

These are the silent helpers who guide us on our journey to find the keys to knowledge. They live in kindness and work their magic for all who know their secret. Many search, but few find the way. They cross-mountains, ford streams, travel for endless distances in search of the secret but do not find it.

They experience life's pleasures and pains, living life to the fullest in human terms, but still feel empty; although not sure what they are empty of.

Many years, perhaps lifetimes are spent in pursuit of the illusive and when all effort is exhausted and their soul cries out in surrender, then are they ready to hear.

At first the call is like a distant wind blowing through the grasses of a high meadow. It is warm and inviting but mysterious and still far away.

As one's focus is sharpened by life's apparent difficulties, its melody becomes clearer and more distinct. There is something familiar about it.

Just hearing it brings joy into one's life, a joy which is shared with all whom we come in contact with. The more it is shared the louder it becomes.

Its message is loud and clear, but not in words. Rather it is like an ancient song whose rhythm and melody vibrate through the entirety of creation.

We listen with rapture and know that we are home. We wonder how we ever lost it and where it has been throughout the millennia. But we know in our hearts that we have always carried it inside us. We merely misplaced it temporarily. There it has waited patiently for us to again find the quiet in which it resides. It watched as we chased the wonders of the world, knowing we would return one day. It rejoiced in our successes and wept with us in our confusion, but it never lost faith in us, for it knows the truth.

This truth is not obscure and esoteric, but easily accessed and applied on earth and in heaven. It is not for the select few, but for all and in all.

We are it. It is not merely a concept to be contemplated on Sundays. It is a living truth, in all and of all that exists. It is our very essence, our very being.

It is the energy of the universe, unlimited and majestic, yet so much more. We touch it through our goodness. We become it through our joy.

We share it through our kind thoughts, actions and words. Through sharing it increases. It is our choice and our inheritance.

It was born in light and it resides in light. Through the light of our joy it is revealed. Through sharing it grows. It illuminates our journey's path, smoothing the way, and leads us to an end, which upon arriving we recognize as where we began.

We were lost, but now are found. We were blind, but now we see. By choosing compassion, we have reunited with Truth and know it as the home we never really left.

That Easy and That Hard

The power is already ours. It is within us, given to us at the dawn of time. The power is love and it is only unleashed by love. When we love we unite with the power of the universe. Our challenge is to open the floodgates of love wide enough to let it come streaming forth. Loving words, thoughts and acts open the gates. The more we love the wider they open. Criticism, fear and hatred shut them tight and surround us with darkness. Our job on earth is to love and true loving is giving. True giving is selfless love. It is that easy and it is that hard.

Robert H. Wellington

Inspiration

Glory twinkling through the morning dew.

Fragrance floating over summer breezes.

Colors too innumerable to count.

The sun's warmth, the spectacle of light.

Leaves quake and shiver in the wind.

Mirrored images at sunrise on still lakes.

The majesty and power of a spring storm.

Life giving waters calling forth the earth's bounty.

Plenty for all who fill only their needs.

Knowing our place within its majesty.

Seeing ourselves within looking back into our own eyes

And recognizing our oneness with the mystery.

This is the key which lets us into His secret garden.

This is the pathway which leads to His open heart.

We must look and in looking we must see.

Balance

Balance, true balance is known in the heart but cannot be spoken. Its example shines forth brightly, but its splendor cannot be put into words. It exists within the heart of the Holy Spirit. It is a knowing and a natural kindness. It is its own reward as lack of balance is its own punishment. It is the manifestation of that high state where words cannot follow and must be left behind, where thoughts cannot form and only the heart may know its passion and truth. Balance is not a system of rules, however well intentioned. It is truth itself which can be lived only when our will is transformed into His. Balance is the way and the goal. Balance and Love are brothers on the path and cannot exist apart from one another.

Robert H. Wellington

From the Mountain Top

We, too often have the uncanny ability and propensity to make our problems seem much greater than they really are. By focusing intently on our problems we lose perspective and soon our rational mind has only the problem itself from which to base its comparisons. This is the way the mind works and to protect the mind from this folly we must maintain our balance and perceive worldly issues from a higher point of view. From the mountain top the entire panorama can be viewed and clear thought will always be the result.

All Are Family

See all people as brothers, sisters, sons, daughters, mothers and fathers. Feel their goodness in your heart as you come in contact with them. Become centered in your own true nature. Love constantly because it is a gift to God which flows back to you many many times over.

Robert H. Wellington

All from You (A Prayer)

All that I have you have given to me. All that I am you have bestowed upon me. Your gifts are of yourself, your love, your strength, your wisdom, your virtues. The more I am, the more I am of you. The more I am of you, the more I am and the clearer I see that which is and has always been. I expand with my love. When I am touched by beauty I have become larger though you. When my heart leaps with joy, it is because you are filling me. When love guides me I am holding your hand. You are not separate from me. We are one. We must truly realize this to make it so. For it is a fundamental truth waiting only for recognition. May I always be cognizant of this, may I know that the I is you and that the little I is your servant whom you love.

The Choice is Ours

Through perfect peace and balance one finds the silence within. Be still within, find the point of perfect balance and you will find loving peace, unlimited refined energy, and the joy of God which is His gift to all those who seek. This is the point of all potentiality, the womb of creation. This is where the Father, with us by His side, spoke the word. This is the point where He breathed upon the waters. This is where He set in motion the vibrations of creation and with it time. In the silence all potential resides. His Love invites us daily to rediscover His peace, long ago lost in the fog which separate thinking built (in fact we built) around us. He invites us to again co-create with Him and in so doing reconnect with infinite bliss as we experience Him, His creations and through us He enjoys all that He has made. His plan is so perfect, for only perfect stillness knows and can find the source. Only a Loving heart can find the stillness. Thus, Love is the way and the key to the Kingdom. Only Love can create and only Love is created. Love creates Love. That is all there is. Evil cannot enter this place for evil does not exist in the presence of Love, just like darkness does not exist in the presence of light. Although evil seems to exist in this world, if we look with clear eyes we see it is only in places where we have chosen not to Love. God gave us choice so that we can choose to experience Him on earth and in the experience learn who we really are. If we choose not to love, to judge others, to see ourselves as separate and alone, we turn from the light and evil takes up residence in the void. Choosing Love annihilates evil like a light does darkness and in so doing we turn back towards the Father and home.

In the early morning we might say, "I am your servant Father, a wisp of your energy swirling in space-time. I am creation set in motion by you before time began. I can never be separate from you for you created me from the peace which is you, but you also gave me choice that I might choose you and in so doing discover myself. And just as I experience through you, you experience through me; in essence, God experiencing God through God which is our greatest joy. I am not God in a human sense, but I am of Him and in perfect surrender, which is my choice, I merge back into the infinite which is Him, where all mysteries are revealed. I am home, the center, the circumference and all points between.

That which is within can be shared without, if we choose to let it be so. That which is beautiful and pure can be spread through out the chaos, sharing its peace and perfection with a tired world. We have only to surrender, letting Him pour into our being. By surrender the seeming chaos within is no more as His Love instantly fills the apparent void, a void which existed only as our temporary choice. His Love is an energy which must flow to be and so we must share it freely, letting it flow without restriction to all. The source is unlimited, only we restrict its flow when we suffer with a misguided freedom of choice. The conduit through which our Love flows narrows only to the degree that we have separated ourselves from the One. Egos, by their very nature, live in a world of judging others, self-absorption, self-centeredness, greed, gossip, anger, and the cause behind all of these, fear. These are the great separators that limit His presence in our hearts. Surrender and separation work inversely to each other in the flow of God's Love; in the establishment of His kingdom on earth. The more completely we surrender, the more we embrace His Love and spread His glory over the world. There is no limit to the flow. Perfect surrender is transfiguration, the goal of all humanity, the gateway home. It is our choice. Once made we begin to clear the dust and cobwebs from memories long forgotten, knowledge indelibly written upon our hearts before the beginning of time. This knowledge was always within us, but covered by the dust of worldly storms and an ego born in separation, the same ego that will die in awakening. This knowledge waits patiently to be found. A loving heart leads one to it as certainly as the sun gives light to our planet. There under a pile of debris it resides, glowing and singing its angelic hymn. Remove the debris and we are blinded by its light, the first principle of creation. It is this light from which the bridge between heaven and earth is constructed. It is this bridge that each will cross on their journey home. It is a jewel buried for millennia, but now found. The ego does not want this treasure found, for the ego was born in separateness and can only exist in its separate delusion. The jewel is Oneness; it is the way. It is the Father within, the light of our true being. It is right inside of each of us, nearer than our very breath. It is one within all of humanity. Only Love can touch it, hold it and share it, for it is pure Love, the Heart of God, all in one, unlimited and forever. Love and it will unfold in you like a nuclear explosion only infinitely more powerful. It is the Child within, that which must be reborn within each of us. See the Child in all and you will know the Child within. See the Child within and you will know the Child in all. Through the Child's eyes you will know Him in all things. We have only to choose, to lay all attachment to the things of the world aside along with the children of attachment. Fear, anger, hatred and unnatural desire are its offspring and these keep us bound to a world of separatism. Embrace the Child within and He will lead you from darkness to light, from sadness to joy, from chaos to peace, from hatred to love, and from judgment to forgiveness. Complete the journey and you will awaken to the knowing that you and the Child are One. You will at first feel it within your heart, then your whole being and finally in the infiniteness of His essence, in all things forever. The choice is ours.

Robert H. Wellington

The Source

He knew himself within the wind

He greeted it, it greeted him

He knew its touch and through it shown

That he could never be alone

With velvet passion it caressed

With stormy anger it obsessed

Unceasingly it drives the clouds

It wears the weather as its shroud

Creating ripples on the sea

And flickers of the aspen's leaves

It's searing heat or cooling touch

Is just its way in giving much

To each who know the inner peace

Where soul resides and joy's released

What is it that will know its own

What is it that through light alone

Will shred the dark and mend its tears

And before heaven will declare

That all is one without division

Just one cause and just one vision

Creating earth and wind and sea

Creating life and you and me

And placing us within its fold

Eternal partners we are told

Before beginning, after end

Beyond horizon, round the bend

A journey home transcending ages

It is His book, we turn the pages

Drumbeats

Rustling trees, summer breeze

Calling us to recognize

In the dance, take a chance

Live on earth but touch the skies

Feel the ground, hear the sound

Sacred drumbeats from within

Find the bright inner light

Once you know then you begin

Know the toil, work the soil

Smallest efforts find reward

Loving feet know the beat

To the truth you journey toward

Joyful time, life sublime

Dare to live a life complete

You are proof of one truth

Love can never know defeat

Robert H. Wellington

Peace

Peace, so patiently it awaits discovery beyond the world of thought.

So quiet, so utterly still it awaits.

It does not hide from us, although we often hide from it.

No thought lurks there for it is all knowledge, all wisdom.

Not a ripple can be seen on its still waters,

Yet one true command from this place of perfection can move mountains.

Hidden behind a curtain of thought we find it.

Its indescribable beauty beacons us to step within its all encompassing embrace.

Warmly it surrounds us, all earthly sounds and chaotic vibrations left behind.

We feel at home for here we truly are.

In perfect stillness we know beginning and end in present alone.

All is peace and the joy of knowing that nothing is separate.

The world of thought created a dream world in which we sleep thinking it reality.

Finding peace we awaken.

It is this simple and this hard.

It is the only reality.

Life without peace is only a dream.

A Marriage Blessing

Marriage, the joining of two, so much more than one plus one.

United through the heart, go forward together but not in each other's shadow.

Rather let your Love expand the reach and wisdom of the other,

So that all whom you touch are blessed. These blessings are returned to you tenfold.

Love unites us with God and thus a loving marriage becomes a communion with him and all who come into your life. Heaven and earth rejoice in your love.

Many experiences you will have together, some exhilarating, some painful,

but all a blessing if met with Love.

We learn about God through these experiences and what a joy to have a friend to experience them with.

How you respond to life's curves impacts all those around you.

These are life's lessons, comprehensive and without rules except the rule of Love

Lessons learned with Love are wings for our feet and hurry us toward greater understanding.

There is no greater incubator to understanding than the experiences of marriage and raising a family.

Beginning with the up close and personal interaction of two adults, followed by the immeasurable joys and occasional pain of raising children, and ending with the clearer recognition of the beauty of the partner you have shared most of your life with.

Yes, there are joys, endless joys which when experienced through a loving marriage lift us right to and through the gates of heaven.

And yes there might be some pain, sometimes excruciating to our humanity.

But when trials are faced with love we see that the knives of pain merely hollow us so that we can hold more Love.

And so in a real sense our defeated pain becomes our joy

Love is the key, a constant giving and forgiving love,

A love which will reward you each day with unexpected blessings.

This I wish for you and this I pray God will shower upon you.

It begins with your choosing Love and it ends, well it never ends.

God bless this marriage

Innocence

Our future depends upon our finding the innocence of our beginning. Young children look at you and the world around them with no preconceived notion. Without judgment, they experience their new life and pure love shines through them. Looking into their eyes we see heaven on earth. They live in joy and perfection. They live in the present. As we grow up the world corrupts this innocence or so it would seem. The demands of the world, food, clothing and shelter cause us to focus elsewhere and our natural innocence slowly fades. Yet it is this innocence, which we must find again if we are to return home and reconcile with the Father. In a very real sense innocence regained allows us to complete the journey of the Prodigal Son, a journey we all seem to be taking to one degree or another while on earth.

But how do you find innocence lost? The world seems to rip it from each of us and then conceal it under years of silt and rubble until no trace can be seen. We came in innocence and the world took our very essence from us. In our deep subconscious, we condemn the world for this betrayal. Even though hidden by the world's illusions we know something special is still there somewhere, something that makes us whole and fills the emptiness. It is that special something which we spend our lives looking for. We try to fill the emptiness with worldly pursuits for surely the answer is out there. Whether money, passion or power, we feel if we only had a little more we would somehow be fulfilled. But the world cannot fill the emptiness. In seeming hopelessness, we cast blame on all and in so doing merely increase the illusion which hides the truth from us. The world's depression manifests from this illusion of hopelessness. We wonder, "Is there hope. Can we emerge from this deep pit where all is dark?"

The answer to this question is a resounding yes. Emergence from blindness to sight simply begins with forgiveness. Forgiveness is the key given by the Holy Spirit to find our innocence. When we merge with our innocence, there is no longer any need for forgiveness, for innocence is non-judgmental, but in the beginning there must be forgiveness. In innocence, we know God and become one in His truth. In innocence we leave all judgment to God. Leaving judgment behind we forgive the world. Innocence is the purity revealed within the heart. In innocence, we know God and return home.

A Life Well Lived

She travels free with the wind and the sea
and the spirit that speaks with its own.
Now unfettered by time, she rests in the sublime;
calmly waiting for you and for me.
Look with eyes to above, there you'll find a white dove
and a glow where the answers are known.
Seek the hand that's outstretched, beaconing to the quest
that enables the blind ones to see.

For a life that's well lived, find the heart to forgive,
for without it we all go astray.
Innocence that is sweet, known in those that we meet,
will touch all with its heavenly glow.
To a heart that is pure, narrow ways become sure,
touching many along journey's way.
Even those unaware find a life of despair
disappears by the touch of Joy's flow.

So we celebrate life and its lessons and strife
that we might regain memories lost.
Memories of His realm and our place on His helm;
our true home which is free from all fright.
Just a haze since the fall, but still all hear the call;
we must find it whatever the cost
Hush the storm that's inside, where the false tries to hide
His true wisdom and spirit's insight.

Robert H. Wellington

Never Alone

I sit among the trees at sunrise feeling at home.
I close my eyes, my mind becomes quiet,
The wind cools my skin and welcomes me.
Silently I hear myself whisper, "Thank you."
The birds sing to one another and to the awakening day.
The wind rustles the leaves.
I am thankful, I am at peace.
My body communes with nature.
My heart soars, for I am beginning to see.
The wind caresses me but not as something separate.
For, I am the wind.
The sun warms me but its rays are not separate from me.
My Heart touches all as I am touched by all.
It reaches out and is answered.
I become all as all becomes me.
Was I ever separate?
Many facets, one truth,
Shining like a perfect diamond.
I experience the sun, as the sun experiences the touch of my skin?
Barriers dissolve as I recognize its conscious awareness.
Does the sun also seek to know?
Does the galaxy likewise strive to know a conscious universe?
Does awakening have an end?
The thought stirs something deep within.
Deny them and we are caught in a mold.
Embrace them and discover the dreamer.
Feel the wind and sun and rejoice.
For it is only you longing to be recognized.

Timeless

Timeless, eternally present comprising all

Powerful, blinding in brightness, healing the fall

Gently embracing, renewing, singing its song

Telling its story to all that was hidden so long

Melting the chains of my bondage, helping me see

Removing the shackles that we might forever be free

Waiting so patiently, knowing that truth will soon come

Awakening realization when our work is done.

Robert H. Wellington

Water and Love

Water, the fluid of life, sustaining, revitalizing, enriching all that lives.

Without it life lies dormant, its potential hidden, seemingly non-existent.

But when the rains come, life's potential is made manifest

springing from what had seemed to be lifeless.

Life was always present, but waiting for expression.

As water invigorates life, love invigorates the spirit establishing it on earth.

Spirit was never absent, it merely awaited a decision to love.

A choice, given to us at the beginning of time.

As water begets life, love is spirit made manifest.

Forgiving

Ask the heavens for forgiveness and it is granted

Forgiveness given must be shared

Not a piece should be kept, all must be given.

Yet somehow when shared we have more

Again it is shared and again we are filled and overflowing

Through sharing the gift expresses its unlimited nature

With each sharing it grows

When not shared it disappears

To have, we give without expectation of return

The purity of the gift is reflected in its infinite manifestation

Robert H. Wellington

Relinquishing the Throne

I say in my heart, "Lord come, take your rightful place

on the throne which is my very essence."

You answer, "Of course, but my gentleness can only take its place on the Throne

upon your relinquishing it."

"You must remove yourself completely that I might flow into your heart

and lift you back home."

And I say, "But Lord, how do I remove myself completely?"

And you whisper, "By becoming me."

In the Silence

It doesn't happen in the brain; it happens in Silence.

Silence is where we truly abide, between the thoughts, where pure consciousness expresses itself.

During silent moments, we must not anticipate a revelation in the brain for the brain has little to do with enlightenment.

In the Silence, revelation is the recognition that we are the consciousness we find there.

Go and enter the Silence.

When in quiet contemplation know that much is happening

The brain however plays no part except to remain silent and be as a witness.

It is our faith that enables us to become One.

This is experienced on a level well beyond the brain and its comparative thought capabilities.

This happens in Spirit, in the Light.

Bringing it back and sharing it with the world is our gift.

Sharing is the natural result of being, for by being we must share. They are inseparable.

Have faith when you enter the Silence.

When you return to the world, let your transformed consciousness shine through your Love.

This is true giving. Upon awakening it is as natural as breathing.

Robert H. Wellington

Free Yourself from Restrictions

So restricted is the world we hold ourselves within.

So constrained and small is the world we have chosen.

Why do we make such choices when our true realm is so beautiful that human words and concepts cannot begin to describe it?

Like a prisoner in a cell, we think the four walls, floor and ceiling that comprise our boundaries are all that is.

One step outside our prison walls and an explosion of consciousness takes place upon realization that there is so much more.

Some would run back into the safety of their cell out of fear, postponing their awakening to a future time.

Others choose to soar with the realization that they have been asleep, but now are awake.

These wise ones leave the dream behind and merge with the Light.

While some shield their eyes from the light, others after searching every corner of the world to no avail finally turn inward and in the Silence begin the journey home.

In the Silence they rediscover their connectedness to all as their unlimited nature is revealed to them;

A truth they have always known but had temporarily forgotten.

The truth was always within reach but hidden behind a curtain of thought and illusion created by an over active brain, an illusion humanity has mistaken for consciousness.

Quiet the brain and the self generated illusions must dissolve, revealing our true nature.

The Prayer and the Answer

Once in a dream I called your name.
You healed me, dissolved my shame.
Hearing your hymn, I find my way.
The night I knew turns into day.
Where once was dark you gave me light.
All my fears, flee from your might
You know my mind as I request.
Gently guide me on my quest
Spirit within is now set free.
Never were you away from me.
Touching my heart I know your love.
Residing there, the gentle dove.
Cleansed by your blood that I might know,
true love's healing gentle flow.
Blessed by your love that I might see.
I will always exist in thee
You are the answer and you are the prayer.
Always with me, while everywhere.

Robert H. Wellington

Spirit

Leaves blowing on a crisp bright day

Witness the breeze which we do not see

Sometimes gentle, sometimes a tempest

We do not see it yet it is there

We feel it rush by us

We see it in the ripples of a quiet pool

We know it is there yet we do not see it

Joy in the eyes of a child

Witness the Spirit which we cannot see

So powerful yet always gentle

We do not see it yet it is there

We feel it rush through us

Quickening our Soul during a quiet moment

We know it is there yet we see it not

It is there exposed for all who look

Yet too many do not try

Still it is all there.

Flickering Light

Flickering light, steady now
Work to do, fields to plow
Furrows to seed, light to sew
Steady now, Love must grow
Shining from a heart so pure
Where no darkness can endure
Spread your rays, across the fields
Warm the soil, increase the yield

Robert H. Wellington

Wonder

The wind whispering through the leaves causes me to stop in wonder.

A mountain stream, sometimes roaring with winters thaw, sometimes a gentle trickle calms my soul.

Sunshine working its way through the forest's canopy, flickering upon the ground speaks to something deep within.

The beauty of a pristine northern lake sparkles in His infiniteness.

I watch as wind waves and sunlight dance together.

All are wonders that hold the answers to a great mystery if we take the time to observe and listen.

All a part of us as we are a part of them.

The power and majesty of nature's wonders greet us as brothers and sisters.

Joy explodes within as we recognize our kinship.

Man and nature created through the one Will for each other's pleasure.

Listen to nature's song and begin to tap life's abundance.

Know that the wind is caressing us as it moves past.

That the sun warms us and lights our way with the joy of a mother looking over her children.

Know that the waters cleanse, cool and nourish us with a conscious joy.

There is no limit to nature's sharing, for in sharing it completes itself.

Just as we are completed by sharing.

The wonder of Life is His gift.

We have only to reach for it and He will place it gently in our outstretched hands.

Surrender

Open your heart, lay aside fear
Let your light flow, surrender is here
Silence the noise, within the mind
Choose to be free, joy you will find
Turn from all dark, bright is the way
No longer lost, night becomes day
Do not react to thoughts without
Listen in quiet, let silence shout
Do not be swayed by the dark's pleas
All must surrender from upon knees
Only your quiet can save the world
Chaos of lost ones, obscures the word
Choose His direction, and hold steadfast
Silence will show present from past
When chaos surrounds, become a rock
Choose to be like Him and save the flock

Full Participation

I sit among the trees feeling at home. I close my eyes, breathe deeply and quiet my mind. The wind blows past me cooling my skin and welcoming me. I send back a thought of appreciation. I hear the birds singing to one another and to the awakening of the day. The wind rustles the leaves and reminds me that Autumn is here. I am thankful for this moment. I am at peace. My heart soars. The wind caresses me, but I am the wind. The sun warms me, but I am its light and its warmth. My consciousness touches all as I am touched by all. I am no longer separate. I never was. I become all, as all becomes me. We experience each other and recognize that we are experiencing our self, the One, many facets of the one truth. The many facets come together as a perfect diamond. I experience the sun and the wind as they experience me. I have traveled through Love to reach this consciousness of truth. I choose it as it chooses me. I am in all. All is within me. This is the wisdom. One has only to choose it.

Giving

Too often we focus on receiving when giving is all we really have control over. All that we receive has already been given. By giving, we choose to accept this gift. Giving and receiving are one and the same, for by giving we receive. There is no separation in the two, only in the choice. The choice God has given us is whether to give or not give. It is a choice for Him. Instantaneously, upon choosing to give, we receive. It is His law and His pleasure.

Give of your Love for what you give you truly are. We have been given this life, mind and body that we might learn who we really are and in the knowing expand His kingdom. Don't separate your consciousness from your gifts of Love, for that gift is you. Let your consciousness expand with your gift and reacquaint you with your own Oneness. We are not these bodies or these thoughts. We are the Love we give. Our body and brain are merely witnesses to our giving. In the silence we remember that our true nature is Love. Through the choosing it expands and we become creators. Not side by side with God, but as an inseparable part of Him for he is Love. This is as it has always been, we have only to remember.

There is no real difference between giving Love and being Love except as a matter of degree. Being Love is the most perfect expression of giving Love for one cannot be without giving. Love only exists when given. Even if we are only feeling appreciation for a beautiful day, we are flooding the airways with loving vibrations for all to share. Jesus' very shadow healed. He was all Love which was given freely to all whose hearts were open enough to receive it. A loving heart leaves an endless stream of good deeds in its wake, which forever ripples through time. Surrender to it and the doors of heaven must open for you even on earth.

Robert H. Wellington

Quickening

I know you are there waiting for me to let you in.

Standing there in your perfection, knowing every particle of my being, every thought yet you do not judge me.

You wait there patiently, waiting for me to notice you and invite you in.

The chaos of the world confuses me and obscures my vision, but I know you are near.

I close my eyes, quiet my mind and repeat your prayer.

You move closer to me.

In my joy I bless the world and you course through me like lightning through the air.

For a precious moment all is clear and I send your love to all corners of the world trusting it will find all those in need.

It must be given for that is your way.

You have given me the choice, but upon choosing you perform the labor.

I as a witness become one with pure joy for you are joy and you flow through me to all who are seeking.

You flow through all who have truly chosen.

Those who have surrendered see the truth in all things and know your oneness for they see through your eyes.

Overcome with joy a song of praise is heard coming from my lips.

It must be so for it is you and all who choose are carried to infinite heights.

My body shakes as you flow through me, cleansing me as you cleanse the world.

Purity and perfection flow through me for they are you and in surrender I become them.

I become one with you, inseparable and complete.

The Heart

The heart sees what the senses cannot. The heart is aware in a manner foreign to the senses. It is constantly aware of its connection to all things, only we often do not pay attention or have not learned how to see, listen and know through the heart. It is a matter of focus. When we feel love we are listening to our hearts perceptions. It is an all encompassing and embracing feeling in our breast. With a little practice we can constantly communicate with and through the heart. The heart reaches out to all things for it knows it is consciously connected to all things. Those who are sensitive know and feel this connection and communicate through it. It is the pathway between heaven and earth and always open. Follow your love and it will reveal this pathway. Listen to it, know your oneness with it, share it and watch as heaven unfolds on earth.

Fear

A life that reaches out to others is a life well lived. A love which is shared is worthy of its name. Life's joy is boundless if we choose to make it so. Keeping joy to ourselves or within a small group of loved ones restricts it. Spreading joy is limited only by the degree of sharing. Unlimited sharing is unlimited joy. Fear causes one to withdraw to perceived safety and this is restrictive and contrary to unlimited joy and a bountiful life. Fear is the great obstruction to the gift of life and therefore has no place in true living. There are many types of fear, fear of not going to heaven, fear of failure, fear of or for others. The list is endless. Live a loving righteous life and there will be no room for fear.

The Battle

There is much work to be accomplished. Darkness appears to be overwhelming the world or so it would like us to believe. Love is the army that will defeat darkness. The lines are being drawn. Depraved troops led by darkness are using illusion to fool and snare their victims. It is time to put fear and selfishness aside. It is time for love to reveal the truth and illuminate the path home. It will take frankness, honesty and strength. Most of all it will take courage, courage to love when illusion has blinded your earthly eyes, courage to maintain faith amid seeming chaos, courage to spread joy unceasingly, freely, and with a deep compassion which will carry you to the very center of His heart. When the battle is over there will only be love. This is as it has always been if we only would see it. Darkness' greatest weapon against us is hiding the truth. Under this veil we are fooled into believing that darkness has a legitimate place. Light is not fooled and where there is light there is no darkness. Light and love are aspects of the same truth. We are filaments through which light and love can shine and be transmitted to earth. We must prepare the way by shining as brightly as we can. In this way all shadows will be erased, and darkness removed. This is our purpose in life. What our vocation is, is not important as long as it is Godly and our light shines wherever we are. In this way we can inspire and nurture the world. Our light lights others, each shining with their unique expression which together blend into a light so glorious that words cannot describe it.

Stillness

Stillness, how I love the stillness of the early morning. He is in the stillness. How reverent the stillness is. From the stillness comes the awakening, as life greets the morning light. As the sun rises it quickens the air through its warmth and gentle breezes begin to move through the forest. The animals begin their morning activities and calls echo though the still air. The beauty and joy I feel this morning flows through me and from me. The beauty I see is a reflection of the joyful tapestry within. The beauty outside and inside reflects each other, each enabling the other to be more abundantly revealed. When we express our internal beauty and joy, the beauty all around us is seen with corresponding intensity. This is the gift, the reward and the nature of love. Love is reflected in love. From the greatest to the smallest this is true, as it always has been and always will be.

Love the Creator

By loving we create. True love shared results in more love. When two people truly love they are nourished, refreshed and invigorated by their love. Likewise, when one feels deep appreciation for natural things (perhaps a tree or flower) our joyful energy is increased and the tree or flower benefits also. Love is a special kind of energy. Whenever one gives love he or she has more as does the person that receives their love. Love is not a zero sum game. Rather it is a creative energy. Love creates itself and manifests on earth and spiritually in all its diverse and varied beauty. "Whenever two or more of you are gathered in my name, I am there." When two are gathered in the name of love more love is the result. It is a wonderful thing. It is the cause and the purpose of life.

Renewal

Water, so pure and beautiful, is constantly renewing itself though evaporation and the rains. Water which stands still for very long soon becomes stagnant. Water which flows is forever refreshing itself. It is this way also with people and the energy of love. Love held still or kept to oneself soon spoils, but love shared is constantly renewed. Water is life to the body. Love quickens the soul.

To the Children

Find the joy within, serve it and all else good and true will come to pass. Seek the joy of learning and good grades will be yours. Seek the joy of competing in sports and athletic skill will be yours. Seek the joy of friendship and popularity will result. Joy and love are the cause of all things and they can only be found, within you. Looking outwardly reveals no truth. One must look inward to find the light and once found it must be shared through your joy. In a very real sense joy is a pure energy. This energy is the cause of all things. When one seeks the cause, all good effects will come to pass. Do not worry about the effects. They have no power. Only the cause, love and joy, leads to happiness. God bless those who shine with joy, for their light is a temple for all. A kind thought is the breath of an angel clearing the way. A kind word is the hand of an angel straightening out the traveled path. A kind action is an angel working through us and giving love to the world. Kindness has at its root pure joy. So also does gratitude and forgiveness, compassion and selflessness. Joy gives form to chaos and reason to our lives. Through joy we touch the meaning of our existence and begin to know God. Joy is love, thus joy and the Father are one. By becoming joy, we become one with the Father. Joy is His gift to us and oneness is our destiny. We have only to reach out and take it. No one bestows it upon us. Each of us individually must make the choice. Look within, find your unlimited strength and become your true Self.

Growing Up

The trials of growing up are many and challenging. Some of us learn how to cope with the difficulties, but like a buoy on the ocean continue to be buffeted by waves and tides. A very few learn the secret of life and these control their destiny and calm the rough seas. The formula for a happy productive life is so simple yet only a handful among all humanity embrace it and become one with it. The challenge is to put selfishness aside and merge with a greater truth. But selfishness in all its subtle forms seems so tangible, and love so etheric that we are reluctant to release it and let love take its rightful place on the throne of our being. Let go of the baggage of the world, hold firmly to your inner joy and dive into His awaiting arms. He will catch you and give you renewed life. Love and spread your joy. In this way you are one with Him and firmly upon the path which leads to His promise, the promise of the keys to the Kingdom.

Appreciation

When you are at home, be at home for your family. Be accessible. Let your heart lead the way. Appreciate the wonder of each day. Know yourself to be a part of it. Let go of all judgmental thoughts. Soar with your appreciation of the wonder of it all. Be healed of all that holds you back. When your attitude becomes one of appreciation rather than judgment, your soul sings and blissful joy courses through your veins. Your heart leaps and you know you are truly home.

Attraction

Through joy we live each day fully.

Through love we maximize the present.

Through goodness we attract all that is good to us.

Through being we become the truth.

Do not fight the joy that is within you.

Neither should you force its opening.

Rather let it bloom like a Lilly in the sun, and

your fragrance will draw to you all that is good.

Recognize this fact and it will be so, for in truth it already is.

The Gift of Giving

Life is a constant and ever-present opportunity to share your love. See each day as the precious opportunity that it is. It is a gift from heaven. Not sharing your love is a cause of stress, and congestion and ultimately disease. Sharing, giving and forgiving leads to freedom, health and ever-lasting joy. See this truth and know the Father.

Robert H. Wellington

Homeward Bound

Fly, for the winds beckon you unto them.

Soar, for it is your destiny.

Rejoice in all good fortune, yours and that of others, and

the world will never disappoint you.

It is our choice whether we surf the waves of life or are crushed under them.

We are one with our brother.

Only our bodies are separate, our spirit is the same.

Recognize this and become free.

Transfiguration is merely the total embrace of the truth that has always been,

the journey from blindness to sight, the journey home.

The Way of the Heart

How precious each life is. How infinitely precious. We have each been given a body so that we may communicate with the world and in the deepest sense of communion, know Him, our Father. We should never hate the world or fear that somehow it separates us from God. God is in all things and the world is a great university through which we learn to recognize God and to know Him. Ultimately when true revelation comes, we realize our oneness with Him.

Look, see, feel, think and act through your heart. This is the key to knowing Him. Our hearts always know. They cannot be deceived. The intellect is the servant of the heart. The intellect is a wonderful tool through which the heart's loving direction is established on earth. How precious life is. Christ watches us from every leaf, insect, animal, river, mountain and all that is. Every breath is holy. The earth upon which we place our feet is holy. We walk the holy path, the razor's edge, the narrow way when we become conscious of this and let the truth which sleeps within each of us awaken and take its place on the throne of our hearts.

How extraordinarily precious life is.

The Razor's Edge

To be a healer, we must first heal ourselves. Only then can we take the light of healing out into the world to heal others. To heal ourselves we must find our love inside, follow it to the place of peace and silence and be cleansed. The cleansing process is one of recognizing who we really are and then becoming that truth in the world. It takes only an instant, a holy instant. Love is the guide to this miracle. Follow it, become it, for the miracle has already happened. It awaits only for the recognition that it is forever so. It is the awaking from a dream of unreality to reality. Your search for truth will not be successful until you become truth. It is the becoming which is the path. It is the effort to achieve awakening which is the razor's edge.

Children

Children are gifts from God giving us hope for the future. It is natural to see the presence of God on the face of a small child. As they grow however, this light may become hidden as growing pains and the self-consciousness of recognizing one's individuality overwhelms the light. Sixth and seventh grade, the early teen years, puberty and social recognition seem to cut the umbilical cord which connected them naturally to Heaven. It is as if some great plan cuts them loose so that they might grow through the process and experience finding one's way home. Perhaps, if we parents, could only recognize this, then we might stop agonizing over our children during these difficult years and just love them. Love them with the unconditional love which they gave to us during their infancy. Only this love can guide them back. Hurt feelings and thoughts of excessive discipline only serve to push them farther from home and us. We participate on this quest together with our children. We, by our actions, can be loving guides or unknowing hindrances.

Teen Years

Reaching a teen is often a difficult task. Love is the only answer, but usually requires a heavy dose of patience. True patience comes from knowing that all must turn out right, that God has a plan which we cannot see until we let ourselves become a part of it, by becoming love. Then healing comes. Love is the life line onto which our teens secretly hold and with which they pull themselves from the apparent darkness of growing up. If we are impatient, we snatch this rope from them and leave them feeling alone. It is only our own fear which is impatient. There is no place for fear in love. They cannot co-exist, for each is a separate choice. Reach out to your children and all with patient lovingness. Your efforts will always be rewarded.

Sleeping and Awakening

How easy it is to forget how much we have to be grateful for. How easy it is to slip into a mode of awareness where all is compared with where it was a few moments before. When we look at something, we should be thinking, "What a wonderful thing it is to see," but we generally think nothing of it. When we write, we should recognize how amazing it is to be able to formulate thoughts into written words which someone else might read and understand as deeply as you did when you composed them? When we touch, do we feel life or just the pressure of touching? Do we try to know the item touched or do we give it only the vaguest of attention? Do we see joy in life or merely the repetitive drudgery of another day? To see, hear, touch and know deeper requires only that each of our precious moments be navigated with a loving presence. We all have this ability, only some have yet to awaken and recognize the gift. The more we love the more it flows though us, and the more we become aware of His mystery.   Life on all its levels is such an exquisite gift. Become present in all you do. A small increase in this loving awareness showers His abundance on the observer and simultaneously on the world many times over.

Robert H. Wellington

Quiet

Quiet, yet extraordinarily alert, aware of the smallest miracles as if one were a part of them (which indeed we are), a leaf quaking in the wind, a mockingbird's song, even a pebble on our path or a small insect going about its business. Each breath one breaths feels as if it were being absorbed and expelled thorough the entire body. The energies all around us are felt and recognized through subtle touch as to texture and essence. The heart reaches out embracing all, giving without thought of return. Compassion flows from one's eyes inviting all to share in the joy of true spiritual love. Our entire body is a conduit through which endlessly, love is received and then given, never being held even for an instant but flowing like the eternal river, without limit.

The Search

The search is for Christ consciousness, the holy grail which all of us at some time must search for, find and become. It is the diamond within, waiting patiently for its sparkle to be freed from the clouds of the ego. Angels whisper in our ears that it lies within our hearts, a priceless jewel, against which all worldly things pale. We have only to let it shine. As we have pursued the desires of the world, we have lost sight of it. It is the innocence with which we came into this world, lost and now search desperately to regain.

The world is the training ground through which we must pass. Love is the wings on our feet which can lift us above the obstacles of this world. Love is the lesson, the way and the goal. Love is Christ. Seek Him through love for they are one and the same. Initially, the seeking requires faith but as love lifts us higher, we will be able to see within and know. Faith will be replaced with knowing and knowing with being. Then our eyes will truly see.

Robert H. Wellington

Wilderness Morning

Light shinning through tree branches reflecting off early morning mists. Dew drops upon opening flower petals. A meadow lark welcomes the sun with its song. Gentle breezes ripple across the lake's still waters and softly touch my face to remind me that I too am a part of it. Pebbles on lake bottoms reflect up to me through clear waters. I wonder at what stories they might tell. I touch the water, feeling its coolness against my skin. I bring it to my lips and it refreshes me. It is now a part of me as it always has been. Everywhere I look life smiles back at me. I lean against a large birch tree and feel its energy flowing up from the ground to the leaves and down from the sun to its roots. On its journey it caresses me. A loon beckons to me in the distance, its mournful cry echoing from afar. I vibrate in the presence of it all. The morning's song is my song. My song is its. The moment has become timeless. Gratitude wells up within me. I am home. It has always been within me. I shall never lose it again.

Charge Us with Your Holy Spirit

Oh Father, help those who search for their life's work to find it.

Help those who have found it to complete it.

Open our hearts and minds that they are forever turned toward you.

Bathe us in the rays of your loving goodness that we may blossom and bloom like the Lotus. Let your beauty radiate through us that we may draw others to you.

Charge us with your Holy Spirit the we may charge others as your ambassadors.

God bless the children through whom you remind us of your constant presence.

Surrender

Surrender is the last great choice on the path to the Father. Such a simple concept, yet such a difficult action. Without surrender there is no awakening, for only the Lord can awaken and He will not come unless invited. This invitation is issued by a total surrender of our little will to His. This simple choice may take a lifetime to embrace. The strength of God comes to us when we have emptied and purified the vessel which is our true Self. Then he will come and fill us with His essence which is His promise. But He will not come before this no matter how hard we pray. Prayer without surrender is not heard. It is His will which makes all things right again and our surrender is required for His will to be established on earth. This is the freedom of choice He has given us, a freedom to love Him and bring Him into our lives, a freedom to put Him first in our activities, a freedom to "live life more abundantly."

His Gift

The time is always now to pray
The world it calls for help today
There seems no hope, the world so pressed
But turn to God and all is blessed
God gave us life so we might know
His love and then with seeds to sew
Bring forth His love to earthly plane
Establish light where once was stain
To live life more abundantly
This was His gift, this was His plea
With naked hand I touch His face
Revealed to me I know my place
I stand not next to, but within
And He in me, no place for sin
In perfect harmony we sing
My soul it soars on perfect wing
He gently lifts me to the sky
Revealing truth, His love the tie
Which holds us through eternity
Close to His heart where we can see
The kingdom which he gives with love
To each of us from high above

Robert H. Wellington

God Bless this Journey

God bless this journey which all are taking with me. God bless those whom I do not see but are there always helping me along the way. God bless my family and friends, co-workers and associates. Thank you for blessing this life and filling it with such an abundance of love. Help me to know you more perfectly each day until that glorious moment when there is only you.

Destroying Evil

If there exists evil in the world, it is evil which we gave life to, and if we are responsible for giving it power, then we can also heal it. We see this many times in the bible where Jesus refused to see evil and it was cast out into nothingness. Our ignorance and energy give it its existence and our wisdom and withdrawal of energy destroys it. But it is each of our choices to accept or destroy it. Even Jesus needed the faith of those who came to Him for healing. Without it there was nothing he could do. "Your faith has healed you," was repeated many times. This is the choice we all must make.

Guidance

Each of us has within a Guide who enables us to see the light and bring it into our life. Our Guide's judgment is without flaw if we but listen. We find it in our heart. In truth it is our very essence, our true Self, and inseparable from the Father. In truth it is pure spirit, one with the Father. Some call it the Holy Spirit, others Atman or the Self. Its name does not matter. Jesus called it the Father and His perfect insight enabled Him to recognize and declare before the world that "I and the Father Am One." Each of us has known this love. Some run from it, some ignore it, but a rare few embrace it and express it in their daily lives. These are the light givers, the messengers from God and the hope of mankind. These light bearers love even when treated badly by the fearful status quo whose eyes ache in the light. But those who resist the light are God's children also and in time their eyes will adjust and they too will begin the journey home to the Father.

Filling Emptiness

Only the Father can fill the emptiness and when He resides within our heart then we truly know joy. Open your heart and let Him flow through and out onto the world. In this way we are doing His will. When we put God first all difficulties begin to fade or are no longer seen as problems but rather opportunities to get closer to God. Walk in His light and all our steps are guided. When we live in His light we touch all those we meet with His light. As we touch others we shine more brightly, as do they, for in giving we grow closer to Him.

Robert H. Wellington

Whispers – I am Never Alone

Whispering through the pines in morning, I am never alone

I am greeted by your awakening
You caress my face and refresh my soul
You are always with me as I move through the forest
You touch my skin and say hello

Whispering through the pines in morning I am never alone

You rustle the leaves and say I am with you.
You blow through my hair and say I love you
I walk the hills with you leading me
You strengthen me with your presence

Whispering through the pines in morning, I am never alone

You cool me in the heat of day and
Bring the pine scent to me
You dry me when I am moist
You push my canoe steadily onward
You delight in giving and ask nothing in return

Whispering through the pines in morning, I am never alone

Timelessness

Timelessness, that brief moment when time stands still is a moment of eternity. When we touch that moment, we are presented with the answers to all mysteries. To these answers we say, "Of course," for we have always known the answers, they were just temporarily hidden from us, so that we might learn how to find them. These truths are presented to all who are seeking and sooner or later we are all seekers.

Robert H. Wellington

Sing Your Song

Do not ever forget who you are. Constantly remind yourself. Sing your song unceasingly. Sing it in the silence of morning. Sing it from the mountaintop at high noon. Sing it in inspiration at sunset. Sing it continuously for you are a child of God and your recognition of this allows Him to work through you. For it is your choice. Sing and know that you are a boundless part of the Father's plan. Sing and know that you are always loved.

See Him

See God in everything and you will never be alone. Hear Him in all things and you will never be without song. Know Him in everything and your life will be filled in ways unimaginable. His joy will embrace every action you take, every thought you think, every word you utter.

The Pain of Compassion

Sometimes our compassion results in intense pain. The natural tendency is to turn from compassion until the pain subsides. But the pain is only a sign of growth. When compassion hurts, we are very close to the Father. The pain is merely an outward sign of inward growth toward a new awareness. Like the serpent shedding its skin, so we too must break out of the old in order to embrace the new. Do not fight the pain. Observe it and let it do its work for in the end a beautiful bridge will be built between you and heaven. Then we will truly shine. Then we will truly be His messenger on earth. Then we shall truly dance.

Thoughts

Thoughts for our loved ones, gentle thoughts
Written here, waiting to be read
Thoughts for our children, peaceful thoughts
Longing to be shared, absorbed and spread
Thoughts for our parents, loving thoughts
Giving and receiving without end
Thoughts for our brothers, guiding thoughts
Helping us to see around each bend
Thoughts for our sisters, sharing thoughts
Stirring something deep within our breast
Thoughts for all families, shining thoughts
There to urge us forward on our quest

www.ingramcontent.com/pod-product-compliance
Lightning Source LLC
Chambersburg PA
CBHW072019070526
44583CB00015B/1544